You are an Artist

Dessert and Nile School of Analysis and Criticism
By: Professor/ Omar M. Saeed

Part 1

-Akownoledge
-table of contents
-Author Purpose and perspective

"We read to know that we are not alone" – <u>William Nicholson</u>

Write until IT becomes as natural as Breathing!!

"Writers are explorers" – <u>Bangambik Hoyer Imana</u>

"Don't be a writer; be Writing" – <u>William Faulkner</u>

"Writing... Reminds us that we are ALIVE and that it is a Gift and a Privilege, Not a Right" – <u>Ray Bradbury</u>

"Writing is the Painting of the Voice" - <u>Voltaire</u>

Dedication

To my family; my wife, Mohamed, Ibrahim.
To the best daughters: Enas, Dr. Amjad and
Dr. ELAF.

Acknowledge
To anyone who help me and to my daughter
Amjad and Elaf.

Book is a publication of:
Create space
49 LaCross Rood
North Charleston This, SC 29406
© 2016 by Omar M. Saeed
ISB # 978-0-692-39372-7

Title: You are an Artist second addition
Author E-Mail-omarkomur6 @gmail.com

You Are an Artist

-This book is designed to understand analysis and appreciate art.

<u>This book divided into seven parts,</u>

You are an artist.
I am an artist! HOW?
Show me

Content

Why am I writing this book?
To appreciate art

The aim of this book is to engage the readers in the process of realizing their innate creativity. The title of the book is to help the reader -You- understand a simple fact: You are an artist.

I ask one question to students and people I meet on the street: "Are you an artist?" The answer most reply is "NO. Why?" They explain, "I am not a singer and I am not a painter." These responses about being an artist are limited. This is why I feel the need to write this book; "*you are an artist*".

The new addition to this book is the Plastic Age in Part 4 'History of plastic term'. This is because plastic is included in almost every aspect of our lives. Plastic surgery in our bodies, in your bag, almost every item contains plastic. Notice the packaging for you food, it contains plastic. Not just packaging food but also objects like perfumes and various liquids. I hope the Plastic Age is added to curriculums in history.

After you finish reading this book, my desire is that you will not only judge art but think about praising art. Realize that you create when you choose what you wear or exercise and even what you eat; creativity is art.

This book's aim is to engage everyone to know themselves as artists, which is demonstrated by the fact that he can practice interpreting art and daily decisions based on taste and aesthetics.

The end to this book is; to appreciate art because "*you are an artist.*"

Message and meaning of the book

Introduction

This book is to prove that everybody is an artist because everyone practices art every day. Also, anyone can judge art and criticize. It is better to create art but even better to write, and talk about it.

It is not hard to prove you are an artist. Talking, thinking and even writing. All this will be easier when you finish reading this book. The reason is that we practice art every day throughout our lives and we don't even realize it. Art is an idea in our mind, feeling in our heart and colors on our body.

Think about one who is not educated and living in small village that creates traditional art, he is an artist. This artist could be in Asia, The Middle East, Africa, or America. We just need to open our mind to what we see on the street, in our house, or in the market or on our body. Thinking like an artist, turns the mall to a museum. Playing is a physical art, and kids starting drawing before writing the alphabet.

Art resides in simply being. Being what? Yourself. The way you walk to the way you talk is a form of physical art. The way you dress is fashion. Every person has a beautiful harmony of traits and characteristics. Since each being possesses its own traits, each a unique piece of art.

Art is all around us. It's limitless and has different forms. It can be a reflection of your personality, with a visual or intellectual representation of what you are from the inside. It can be expressed through painting, sketching, dancing, and singing, playing sports, a musical instrument expression, talking, movement or production. All in all it is part of the six types of art.

1-Visual,

2-Intellectual,

3-Fashion,

4-Physical

5-Technological

6- Natural art.

Desert and Nile

Nature is part of art criticism, desert and Nile is dry and tropical, different climate, resources and environment. As example from North East Africa is a Nubian land.

(The Nubian Desert, northern Sudan, is a branch of the Sahara Desert and a sand valley that runs between mountains and The Nile River.

Inhabitants of the Sahara lead their daily life climbing mountains or going down the Nile's course. Thus, life is divided between the Nile, and the Sahara desert, and mountain). (Alkomur Market. By; Omar Saeed pg.xiv)

The Desert is an element of nature and man's life is formed of various migrations through history. Nature migrated, before man, by the migration of sands from the desert. Water and sand are jostling. So expressions of life refer to the nature. Cultures of nature collide and reconcile on the division of water and sand all over the earth, which consequently enriched the social, literary, and artistic life.

Dear reader, Desert and the water are the constant and variable in the human culture; and they are the two elements that lead meanings of life to origins and sources.

There is information about the effect of the Nile River and Desert's nature on man's life.

(Life cycle goes on every year. Birds come and go. The banks swarm with movement, shouting, noise, jokes, and songs. Steamers depart and anchor. Youths come out leaping off the boats. Women come along with milk. Old men cross Al-Jamam gradually accumulating water and mud. They resist the desertification and Al-Haddam falling of the bank edges into the Nile. Musical tones are played on the river bank between nature and human beings. (AlKomur Market. By Omar saeed.pg.40) Art is an Idea.

Art is an idea, practice and interpretation

A class full of kindergarten students was asked by the teacher to draw any picture from their mind. A student that lived near the Nile River covered the paper with a brown color and on top of the right corner he drew a black line. After five minutes he stopped and said, Teacher, I'm finished. "What did you draw?" the teacher asked. "The Nile River", the student replied.

"But the color of the water has to be blue", he implied.

"No, the river flooded and the water mixed with the mud. This changed the water to the color brown." "What is the dark line on the top right corner?" the teacher asked.

-"It's a Cow"

-What?

-"It is a Cow. It came to drink from the river and as a result, his whole body drowned into the water and the dark line you see there is her tail."

The teacher thought deeply, framed it, and hanged it on the wall because it is an art idea, practice, and interpretation.

If we judge the picture, the Nile River represents the nature, time and season of the flood. The flood is a balance. The picture story is about nature, time and event.

On part three there are three stories; the first one from the Desert, the second from the Nile River, and the third from the land between Desert and Nile, which is brown color and muddy; because mixed by two; sand form the desert and mud from the Nile (Desert and Nile).

You are an Artist

Understand this: you are an artist. This is the most important information you will get from this book. If you practice art every day, or you observe art on your own, you have the beginnings of judging artwork; painting or any two dimensions, intellectual (story or poem).

From this book you will have learned something new, because this book is the connection between the readers and the art work. It is not only opening but to go deep judging the subject.

The school of Desert and Nile analysis and art criticism helps you to judge the artwork by breaking it down, or adding. Expressively, how the art work (story, poem, or picture) reflected on postmodern art works.

Compare and contrast the art works to make it alive, apply it on yourself, and think about how you practice art every day, from hair design to dressing, or shopping, all this related to the art, like fashion from the mall. The mall is not only shopping area, it is a Museum. Basketball and soccer are all types of sports in physical art. The cellphone and the music inside is technological art, from intellectual and natural consider art.

The book observed from two resources Desert and Nile from northern Sudan historical and context idea gives us the fundamental theme of arts.

My teaching in philosophy of art is centered on introducing the great achievements and how they impact world cultures. This is achieved using work that has inspired people of all cultures throughout time. I motivate the people to question the nature of art and culture and its relevance to daily life. This is so the people will be able to answer their questions through creative thinking, projects and presentations.

I encourage all readers to read this book and keep in mind the general picture. Gradually examining the specifications of the subject at hand, to reach a mental vanishing point which is art, and to use this book as a general guide; however I want to challenge the reader to use their everyday experiences in domestic life to the best understanding of art and culture. Through reading, people will know what they practice individually or through group participation. It is to appreciate the aesthetic value of art and culture, through humanities from all over the world.

The above theory is well demonstrated in detail in my book. We should appreciate art, but before we do, we should know what Art is? To answer this question there are six types of Arts; visual, intellectual, physical, fashion, technology, and natural art. Showing images, world maps, and the time line of history the picture of the art frame will be closer to our minds.

This will be done using work that has inspired people of all cultures throughout time. If introduced, beyond the art will acquaint people with the great achievements of the six types of art, and inspire people of all cultures throughout time. In order to answer the question of the five W's; who, what, where, when, and why, this will inspire anyone to question the nature of art and its relevance to daily life in all cultures.

This book will meet General Education Goals (GEG) and Specific History Education (SHE) to enhance the reader which starts from childhood through every day moments from waking up in the morning to the end of the day. All of the above meet both: General Education Goal (GEG) and Specific History Education (SHE).

General education Goal (GEG) and Specific History Education (SHE):-Introduction to appreciate art through writing thinking or practicing and or critique analysis.

Objectives and Outcome:-Under the humanistic perspective, the art will show how important, but unrecognized art is to our lives. Art surrounds every aspect of our lives, but usually we don't realize how pervasive it is. Art is a real subject with its own rules, vocabulary and discipline. There are common elements like what we need to start any of the six types of art, and principles while practicing the six types; it will seem to appear in all art work.

Students will begin to understand the multiculturalism of art in the book. The oral report focuses its attention on the contributions of different cultures to the great paintings, sculptures and works of architecture all over the world. This will become obvious through the understanding of the arts.

What I see is that men and women of every class, color and religion in every civilization have contributed to art. The famous artist's calories and the Museums are capsule biographies that are taught! Art is everywhere completed with standards from not just educated artists in small villages or islands in the middle of nowhere.

Art consists of opening the mind to life and its qualities, activities of art through life receives a clear understanding of the art process, industry and art criticism. Art is our life and art is everywhere.

Examples

Art is very special; because art is everywhere you go. My friend said; I do not think I am an artist, but once I figure out driving my car, getting dress, working, swimming, and drawing, that's where the true artist comes in.

He continued; Art is very special to me, because every time I play outside at the park or watching a soccer game in the stadium, I make sure that art is everywhere.

Painting on paper or canvas and even the human body is a creative art while walking or talking, and because using painting and drawing materials to be creative, with all of the art work that can be combined together. Throughout life, learning all of the techniques of an artist can even help you become an artist.

From this book; the readers will learn six types of art which they never knew before, some may actually know parts of them. Life is creative; nature itself is within beauty, texture, and all kinds of things from any corner is art. Once finished reading this book, I feel satisfied and happy of what I learned about art.

Everyone would love to go out, into the open world, to discover new art visually or intellectually. Art is wherever; because of the materials and the usage items or images of them. Most people don't really notice; because writing and explanation about art is not as big as it was before. It was really important back in the Stone Age and during the Renaissance to the postmodern 2017.

Everyone uses art everyday, due to the technology that has enveloped our life. In the last twenty years, using a cell phone to call, or computers to type, is using intellectual and technological art in the same way. Never get noticed and realized, until you look up to the materials that was used by artists, to find out about the ancient art in our worlds history.

From back then, until now, it is not enough to practically using the art, but supposed to know about history and the time line when that happened. Say I am an artist, because I use my phone and other technological devices every day, but how the home developed from telephones to home phones to cellphones and we do not know what will happen about tomorrow from the researches and the new knowledge.

A student said to his friend: "I am drawing while I'm bored in one of my activities, if I need to occupy my time for whatever reason; I would pull out a book or sketch pad and start drawing anything that comes to mind, like exercise, sports, or nature.

His friend answered: "So anything you do to express yourself, goes on paper. You express how you feel around your surroundings, even playing games."

Sports, acting, or dancing are certain types of arts we mainly know about. Before reading this book, it didn't necessarily make me appreciate art due to the fact that it was something that I had always harbored admiration for, but it did ignite inspiration in which I already had passion for, which motivates me to do what I want to do in my everyday life, with my artistic eyes.

Intellectually; this book is more than anything that has made me fall in love with the idea of art again. The idea was something that brought me comfort, and allowed me to feel more relatable to people who are newly exposed to what art represents in full. But now I feel more comfortable with expressing my ideas of art with those now learning about it, because now the idea and images is more different.

Now the environment is a little greater than an amateur's perspective, now that they have been enlightened. By spending the knowledge of art, it only makes way for one's imagination to run wild in the most positive sense. Say I am an artist because I am a master of creativity, for all of my thoughts related to art are filled with passion.

From this book, I learned that everything could consider art in some way. Before reading this book, I would not have considered most things as art.

However, I learned that there are six types of art; which they are visual, intellectual, physical, fashion, technological, and natural. When I look up in the sky, I try to form shapes on the constellation stars. Whenever I dress myself, I see art because I am matching colors and wearing different styles of clothes. Whenever playing soccer with my friends, I see myself as an artist. We are all artists.

We are all artists because we create different types of art with our talents. Without art, the world would be black and white. Artists painted our life by happiness, such as the way a person dances, sings, or even draws? Artists create and we portray our inside images, based off how we look, smell, talk, act. We are part of art ourselves. Without artists, art wouldn't exist.

Am I an artist? I consider myself an artist, after I reviewed this book. Being an artist takes more than just opening notebooks of sketch paper and opening your mind. In order to be an artist, you need to understand that you are an artist yourself, and everything you do is art. When I am writing on a piece of paper, that is consider a type of intellectual art, similar to physical art.

One day I am outside riding my bike, looking around in the park, to be just in the atmosphere that is art also. I can find that; knowing everything I did is art and inspire everything you do is art and everybody is an artist. Art is everywhere and important in our life. This book taught a lot of things and made anyone realize that they are proud to say I am an artist.

Waking up in the morning and choosing warring clothes or decorating the room is art, and just realizing playing sports is an art and I realized when I did my project on how soccer can be a part of art, I never saw it that way. Art is in our lives and we don't even realize. One of the students wondering and answered; I never saw it that way.

I realized how art is important in our lives and the way we live, we live in art. Thank you the author for such a good book and the real meaning of art. That inspire us to do what we want to do and consider art. Knowing that everything I do art is the most motivating thing in the world. All you need is creativity and motivation to do something and you are considering an artist. So yes, to answer the question, I am an artist.

Over this entire book is great; I learn a lot of things; I didn't think I would learn. Coming into art, I thought art when we would be trying to learn to draw. I was happy to learn that art wasn't just about drawing that there is way more to art. Before I read this book I would have never thought that there are six type of art. I thought that art meant art, I am glad to know the true meaning of art now from this book.

Dear the reader, do you really consider yourself an artist? Yes, you do but in some cases, you really wouldn't. Because you know how to classify yourself as an artist, you might be able to add music taste as an artistic trait. However since music is an intellectual art, you truly appreciating it is appreciating art.

Part 2
What is art?

What is Art?

There are six types of arts.

1-Visual,

2-Intellectual,

3- Fashion,

4- Physical

5-Technological

6- Natural art.

- **Visual:** Visual, arts are forms and Shapes that appeal to the sight making them easier to understand. These art forms are very usual and extremely varied; they can go from a painting hanging on your wall to a movie, when connected to technology. There are two types of visual arts; two dimensions and three dimension art.

Two-dimension arts are flat, could be prints, drawing, painting, petrography and sketch and or collage. Artists choose elements to make their visions appear the way they wish to. For painting, artist use different materials such as watercolors, oil, ink, or pencils, liquid or dry materials.

Three-dimensional art, which can be geometric or organic, these types of arts are defined by the dimensions of high, width and depth. They can have volume, which the amount of space occupied by the form and mass, and is the impression that the volume is solid and occupies space. Some of them are; sculptures, building, cars, and furniture, craft, an object you can see and walk around it.

Visual art can come in two dimensions and three dimensions. Two dimensions are flat paintings such as; landscape, sea scape drawing, photography, sketch, comics, and collages.

Three dimensions; any image can go around it to see the side, front and back. Include buildings (classic, modern, or postmodern), sculptures (Relief- Stand still or Maman), crafts made by human, machine or nature. Cars, train, furniture, bags, or any form object that can walk around it.

Examples: **Visual Art is 2D and 3D
Graffiti Art**

"Graffiti art is a Modern time art particularly consisting of spray paint and Marker, the most commonly used Graffiti materials. In all countries property or painting on without the owner's permission is considered vandalism, which is a punishable crime.

Pointz was recently closed down by the city in 2013. From 1993 to 2013, 5Pointz was a graffiti and street art mecca, a series of evolving murals on the facade of another long island city building, by artist from New York to New Zealand.

Overseen by curator and artist meres one of the paintings went on for 20 years, until the building was sold to a developer who promptly whitewashed all of the murals due to the anger and disappointment of street artists and fans all over the city.

Art could be political, vandalistic or free. Creativity... Graffiti has divided New Yorkers since it first appeared on walls signs and lampposts in the late 1960s. Its ascent paralleled the city's sunken financial fortunes allowing simple markings to evolve into elaborate pieces of art.

The problem was that the best examples were on the sides of subway cars, which the city promptly attempted to eradicate, their attempts thwarted by clever, creative artists and a downtown culture that was slowly embracing graffiti as New York City's defining art form.

"As a statement to visual arts, street art has been established of true expression that originated in the streets of United State of America, in the 1960s and 1970s by rival gangs marking their territory. Graffiti art is painted in the public and is motivated by a preference on the part of the artist to communicate directly with the public at large, turning outside walls to galleries from different artists, some with subliminal message regarding politics and war."

Graffiti then became a movement and as a new culture amongst young people. Given the fact that it was completely illegal to vandalize the streets, the thrill of painting a public wall knowing people will see your art is what motivates street artists to keep painting.

The art community had noticed the evolution of street art that famous street artists' work eventually made its way to galleries and the global art market. Some artists travel to different countries to spread their art and gain attention, some even gain cult-like followings that critics and enthusiasts would travel to the "piece" just to see the street art (Graffiti).

The street art culture had spread throughout every country as well as Europe. On November 9, 1989, the Berlin wall fell and people separated for nearly thirty years by fear, oppression and ideologies were once again united.

This event marked the end of an era in international politics and left an indelible mark on the minds of the German people. Although the Berlin Wall was unquestionably a mental border that divided the German state, the physical structure itself has become an iconic symbol of the twentieth century. Most notable is the graffiti that has become one of the largest ingoing pieces of art in recent history.

The wall now carries messages of hope, symbols of freedom, and images that detail the German experience after World War II. The graffiti on the Berlin Wall has come to represent freedom of censorship, particularly from the East German government, unity in a people torn apart by war, and the fall of the Iron Curtain that divided Western Europe and the Soviet Eastern Europe.

Though these medium artists have impacted world politics and helped to rebuild a nation unto the united developed state that has an influential role in the international community today.

An urban art culture has grown in popularity and adapted various forms; art dealers saw an opportunity to promote a new art form within the white walls of a gallery. Graffiti artists' began to exhibit works in galleries and museums in the 1970s, and subsequently adapted their graffiti techniques into works that fit the gallery mold.

Street art no longer represents the menace it did in the seventies and eighties. It's arguable whether New Yorkers find it offensive anymore. It is part of the romantic, rough-and-tumble past, reserved in museums and coffee-table books.

Street art has been so popular in New York, that there is a legendary place in Queens, NY. Called 5pointz, where artists (mostly known street artists) are encouraged to paint a warehouse where their art is seen by the trains passing by. Now graffiti art is two parts painting on the wall or under the bridge or flat on the street,

so you can see the depth deep in the ground which means it is not flat".
https://hyperallergic.com

Visual: (2-D and 3-D) Another reason why I say art is everywhere because when you step outside into the world and you see buildings, restaurants, buses, and different cars all of those things have a different form of art in It from elements to the principle of art . No matter where you go in the world when you step outside New York City or any town.

That city has one of the best structured buildings to ever be made. I believe that it has the most art because every building and restaurant has different shapes, different colors and the streets and cars are very unique.
Although everyone and everywhere contain their own sense of art in them, whether it's within your outfit, or your body structure, no notices but everyone is an artist in their own way.

- Intellectual:

Intellectual arts refer to any type of logical, rational and analytical representation such as the ability of writing reports, stories, poems, novels , music, research papers, newspapers letters, notes scripts, for movies, calligraphy and many more.

Intellectual: - Writing books, Novels, short stories, poems, music, research papers, thesis one, thesis two, report, journalist, letters notes, and or calligraphy itself. Anyone has a chance; to open up his or her own business and develop his intellectual skill over the time in his life. That is why intellectual art has inspired the artist to write.

Any writing starts the topic with an opining and focus on the statement. They are three writing process

1- General
2- Topic
3- Statement, then what is the important points, stretch each point by using (E-E-E)

A-Experiences from your own,
B-Experience's from books
C- Experiences from other.
It is very important to use inside citation and outside use citations at the end of your writing. To improve the writing let other of different age groups and different point of views and ethics evaluate your writing, from teenage, middle age, adult, and even the kids. The main point writing is passion to express yourself and the main point of your target no matter what style of literature that's used. Any writing should have a purpose that attracts the reader's center of attention.

Persuasive essay process: getting directly to the point because it starts with the statement, the same way of writing one page, (get direct to the point. Persuasive essay going into five liters line (S-R-A-F-T)

S-statement
R-restatement ending with question

A-answer the question
F-for example
T- Tide up the writing in conclusion.

Is journal writing different from the story novels or short story in elements (Time space or paragraph shaping) and motion, is that add value to the subject. Inside the story who is the main character and the characters around him, where is that and when. What type of principle in need, pattern, mood or rhythm?

From intellectual: hardships in his life. He has overcome it all. Overcoming hardships means that the individual has a strong mind. I've been playing football all my life, but I did not recognize the power I had when using my brain. I want to show others that I can actually use my mind, because; it was good has given me, to learn more, and speak less.

I want to open up my own business and develop my intellectual skill over the time in my life. That is why intellectual art has inspired me to write.

Art is everywhere because it is an application of human creative skills and imaginations. Art is typically used in a visual painting or sculpture producing works to be appreciated. However art is practically everywhere you go. An example is when you go to college and meets different people with unique face structures and the way they all are different types of colors and shapes that is going into Natural art.

Shapes is a way because of the lines that make a shape, colors is a way of art because it can come in different shapes, the way you walk and talk is also another way of art because of the way your body moves when you walk, run, jog and any other movement through physical art.

Although everyone and everywhere contain their own sense of art in them, whether it's within your outfit, or your body structure, no notices but everyone is an artist in their own way. Everyone on this Earth is an artist in some way, shape, or form. They just have no clue that they are and neither not educated or having any course because they basic things or daily basis involved art or were in fact considered art.

Student said: - When my art appreciation professor told me that I would see things differently once I finished the course, I honestly believed that he was joking but now I know he was right.

Now I see that everything in this world is art and everything we do is art as well. Furthermore, I'm very much inspired by 3-Dimensional Art because it is amazing to me how much a person can bring drawings and paintings to life; they can take you back to past experiences or capture you in the moment with their artwork. All takes a creative and open minded artist to create a new type of art. A person that has inspired and introduced me to get into three dimension or painting and drawing would be this artist named.

Example: - "Tracy lee stump "she is outstanding artist that has been painting for over Ten years. Mrs. Lee has made lots of people happy because of her works. I am currently study animation art because that is also one of my favorites types of art however I hope that one day I can be just as good as Mrs. Lee. Fashion also helps me to connect with others. For example, I had to pair up with my classmates for a group work and everyone who was wearing sneakers came together. We introduced ourselves and gave each other valuable information on different ways to get cheaper sneakers online.

Additional, we became closer we started to go shopping together. Not only did fashion allow us to express our favorite cosmetics but also allowed us to create lifelong friendship. Like manner.

-Fashion:

Fashion art is the capacity of putting together trending style to make your appearance more eye-catching. Also, there is fashion in makeup, tattoos, hair design, accessories and nails, and everything you use to show your true personality. Just the fact of waking up every day and deciding what to wear, what hair design, and accessories to use, what type of makeup, all of these actions make every human an artist.

Fashion: - Male and female dressing, makeup, hair design, tattoo, henna, jewelries, accessories, Shoes, hats, nailing and fashion shows.

Examples:

The process of writing a song is an art, the process of recording a song is an art, the making of the melody and harmony is also a process of art, the art of music, but the best "Art" is fashion. With fashion, you can tell the world about yourself without saying a single word.

For instance, the clothes I like to wear are Nike sneakers, UGG boots, and Windbreakers which are a sporty kind of style because I am a very athletic person. Just from my clothing and fashion choice, a person crossing my path can determine I am athletic. A lot of stereotyping comes down to fashion. The art of fashion continues to grow but it also repeats itself. Bomber jackets and crop tops you see people wearing now-a-days, seem like a new trend. Newsflash, they are nowhere near new, they are just old ideas/ designs being altered to fit today's society.

In the percent many of us are forced to pull out our old clothing. Sometimes outfits are passed down from generations and it still catches the eye. Fashion is what you make out of it. That is why teenagers are inspired by it. Don't get me wrong, Fashion isn't just about the showcase of your clothes, it's to showcase who the real you is, that's why everybody loves it.

The art of Fashion is on our bodies, it ranges from the tattoos and piercings we have on our bodies to the cars we drive and even the way we walk or the expressions we make. All of those elements are what gets others attention and are a part of the principle of art.

Anyone could say "I am an artist" because the definition of "artist" is someone who creates to express feelings or statements. The artist is a person who sees a shirt and attempts to make it. Not a person that would rather buy it, to avoid the process of creating. The artist has the potential to do anything they put their mind to.

Furthermore, anyone inspired by fashion knows that; once you are dressed nicely and what you are wearing represents your personality, you feel more confident. You walk down the streets like you are in a musical. As stated before, fashion is a way to express yourself and to show your personal style. Fashion can sometimes expose your feelings.

An example; a male wearing a monochromatic outfit can tell you that the person is very simple and straight forward, sometimes, even wise.

Fashion allows me to be myself and have my own personal style without anyone judging me. No one can tell me that the way I am dressed is the wrong way because in fashion there is no rules. Also, fashion is different for each season.

In the summer, I might wear fewer clothes because it is hotter and I don't need to wear layers of clothing. In the winter, I must wear more clothes and add more layers to my outfits. I like the winter because I can add more and look more fashionable. I can wear hats, gloves, a nice coat, boots, sweaters, etc.

Art is also used through fashion. When people dress they tend to have the latest designers and all types of funky colors to bring out their skin tones or a feature pop out more. All the clothes that are made are based off art. First, there is a sketch to plan the clothing's requirements. The materials they need to make the outfit and the different styles that they all use. All the styles are unique and different and they all have a certain type of way of standing out to the media and to the public and shout "who you are".

I am inspired by artists who do great things because I admire their craft and work ethic. Certain artists during the renaissance would put out twenty paintings a day because they really admired and believed in their will to work. They also inspired me to be myself because they had different unique styles to their work, even if sometimes it was not accepted by the crowds. It was rare when you saw identical art.

Art is very important in our lives, especially when we dress. Our dress code has been changing from years to years and it's always something different in what we see in modern days, compared to the old days, it is way different.

That is how you tell there is art in dressing, because you are expressing yourself, for others to see. By dressing up and changing clothes you are creating art within you.

Anybody can be an artist without drawing or painting a picture of sort. Just by simply improvising in the things you like the most, which means practicing art. I could be wrong about being an artist by not applying the idea, drawing design aspect into it.

My own logical opinion, if you want to take the time to learn, draw, paint, or even make abstract form of art, then that's perfectly fine. But I'll be an artist that just adds more to me or the things around me, that makes me a person, as a whole. Last but not least, you are an artist because you practice it in your way in everyday life.

For example; brushing teeth, showering or dressed conceder art, styling of hair design is fashion, washes dishes, typing, printing pictures, and decoration by different materials, driving, eating, and so forth. You will continue being the best artist you can be, because it is what gives you growth and values.

The world we live in is a big museum, give us value. Everything around us is art. Many people do not understand that, anything made with a specific design or feel, is considered a piece of art.

Art is everywhere because it is an application of human creative skills. Art is typically used in a visual painting or sculpture producing works to be appreciated. However art is practically everywhere you go. When you go to college and meet different people with unique face structures and the way they all are different types of colors and shapes. That is art, in a way of life.

Shapes are a way, because of the lines that make a shape. Colors are a way of art, because it can come in different types of shapes. The way of walking and talking is also another way of art, because of the way the body moves when you walk, run, and jog.

Everyone on this Earth is an artist in some way, shape, or form, they just have no clue that they are. Basic things and daily basis involve art or were in fact considered art.

Now I see that everything in this world is art and everything we do is art as well. Furthermore, I'm very inspired by 3-Dimensional Art because it is amazing to me how much a person can bring paintings and drawings to life; they can take you back to past experiences or capture you in the moment with their artwork.

All it takes is a creative and open minded artist to create this type of art. A person that has inspired and introduced three dimensions, painting, and drawing is Albert Einstein which whom is a scientist.

Fashion is the Art appreciated into different ways because: it colors our lives and brings us joy. Fashion also helps the people to connect with others. For example; she said: "I had to pair up with my classmates for a group work and everyone who was wearing sneakers came together". We introduced ourselves and gave each other valuable information on different ways to get cheaper sneakers online. Additional, we became closer we started to go shopping together.

Not only is Fashion art defined as having tattoos, wearing a hat, a bandana, wearing regular jeans, ripped jeans, wearing a long t- shirt, regular shirt, or shoes. Also, when you jump in the pool it makes circles and splashes. Art can be appreciated in many ways.

Fashion allows us to express our favorite cosmetics, but also allowed us to create lifelong friendship. In like manner: look at fashion magazines and see how everybody is so creative and inspiring, that's fashion art.

Art is everything you do, to the way you walk, the way you have individuality when it comes to your hair is set, to the way you have your phone in your hand, and the way you're walking into a car, all represent an art. Art is everywhere, art is us, and we are art.

Art could be seen every day and everywhere: when you're driving, when you're working even, when your home just sitting down watching television or just sitting outside staring at the sky.

Feelings aroused by the touch of someone's hand, the sound of music, the smell of flower, a beautiful sunset, a work of art, love , laughter, hope and faith – all work on both the unconscious and conscious aspects of the self, and they have psychological consequences as well. The smell of a flower, a beautiful sunset, a work of art, laughter, love, is part of art. Just watching the sunset or watching the clouds just form or move is art, the way everything is form.

I have realized that Art Is influential to our everyday life routine. I understand that each movement and choice we make is art. How we think and speak is art. The six types of art are Visual, Intellectual, Physical, Fashion, Technology and Natural Art. Each Art has its own significance. Having a skill of dancing or poetry is Art. Being able to box or make people laugh is Art. Art is what makes any individual unique. It is like a God – given gift.

Each skill that we develop over the years of growing up is an art because of the ability to develop and change. Everybody have the capacity to grow. The humans, animals, machines, are the artists behind the art. Every experience event in his life, expressing himself different and the crowd was amazed. Art has the aptitude to amaze a crowd, in the essence between the six different types of art

Everybody is an artist in many ways just like every single person in the world. He said to his friend: One of the many things that make me an artist is that I love to sing even though I may not sing that well. Singing is considered an intellectual art just like the fact that I use to play the piano.

Like The one who played soccer from a very young age up until junior year in high school or along his life that is considered a physical art. He still plays once in a while but somehow he always ends up getting hurt by spraining his ankles. Its honestly funny how many times he has gotten hurt but he still love the sport because he like to practice the physical Art.

What is art? Are you an artist? What kind of art inspires you? Art is everywhere. Art is a part of our world, from the sea to the forest. The world is art because it is a colorful and like a painting. There is art in what someone choose to wear, the year, how do they do their hair and is a part of our daily lives.

Many people may not notice that art is around them until they sit down and pay attention to the details. The cars people drive is art. For women, there is art in sports which is called physical art. Technology is all around us and it is advancing and becoming better. Many people have technology around them every day. Technology is considered computers, cell phones, cameras, television, etc. It is art because technology helps create films, movies and different types of entertainment for people. There is art is sports people watch which is called physical art. Nature is beautiful and the oceans are as well and are only a form of art. People can paint these things.

Art doesn't have one definition art is everywhere you look. Art is on our clothes which is fashion art, television screens that's technology art, in our textbooks that's intellectual art, in the way we move that's physical art, in museums that's visual art and art is in nature which is natural art.

When you think art is a pictures, painting, and statues. Art is just more than just the name it's self-that's what I love about it art is everywhere in our world. There is not just one meaning to art there's a lot of factors that mean art.

Anyone inspired by fashion knows that once you are dressed nicely and what you are wearing represents your personality, you feel more confident. As stated before, fashion is way to express yourself and to show your personal style. If sometimes, you are feeling sad or down you don't need to dress as nice. An example of an outfit, you can wear is sweatpants, a plain tee shirt, and sneakers. Most of the time when I wear that type of outfit is because I might not be in the mood to dress nicely or I might be too lazy, moods everyone goes through.

Fashion allows me to be myself and have my own personal style without anyone judging me. No one can tell me that way I am dressed is the wrong way because in fashion there is no rules. Also, fashion is different for each season. In the summer, I might wear less clothes because it is hotter and I don't need to wear layers of clothing. In the winter, I must wear more clothes and add jackets to my outfits. I like the winter because I can add more and look more fashionable. I can wear hats, gloves, a nice coat, boots, sweaters etc.

Art is also used through fashion. When people dress they tend to have the latest designers and all types of funky colors to bring out what they are wearing. All the clothes that are made are based off art because the materials they need to make the outfit and the different styles that they all use. All the styles are unique and different and they all have their certain way of standing out to the media and to the public.

I am inspired by artists to do great things because I look back on history and I admire their craft and work ethic. Certain artists during the renaissance would put out twenty paintings a day because they really admired and believed in their will to work. They also inspired me to be myself because they had different and unique styles to their work. It was rare when you saw art that looked completely identical.

Art is very important in our lives, especially when we dress, our dress codes been changing from years to years and its always something different in what we see out moderns 'day compare to the old day is way different from clothing before now and then.

That is how you tell there is art in dressing, because you're making yourself look presentable for the world and how people see you, in different countries people dress differently. By dressing up and changing clothes every day is part of the culture and is making art of you. Anybody can be an artist without drawing or painting a picture of sorts.

By simply improvising in the things you like the most that mean practicing art. I could be wrong about being an artist by not applying the idea, drawing design aspect into it, but it's my own logical opinion. If you want to take the time to learn and draw or paint or make abstract form of art then that's perfectly fine. But I'll be an artist that just adds more to me or the things around me that make me a person I am as a whole. Last but not least, you are an artist because you practice it, in your own way everyday life.

For example: brushing teeth, showering or dressed conceder art. Walking, running reading, styling hair, washes dishes, typing, printing pictures, and decoration by different materials, driving, eating, and so on. You will continue being the best artist you can be, because it is what gives you growth and values.

The world we live in is a big museum, give us value. Everything around us is art; many people do not understand that anything made with a specific design or feel is considered a piece of art. The six different types of art is everywhere.

- Physical arts:

Physical arts are activates which involve efforts and skills to demonstrate your capability of moving. These could be a simple as walking, dancing, running, and as difficult as playing any type of sport: Volleyball, basketball, baseball, football, soccer, golf, boxing, tennis, etc.

Physical:- Physical is for human body movement that are dancing, acting, walking, massage, laugh, all kinds of sports, such as, basketball, volleyball, soccer, football, ping pong, running, swimming tradition games, as well as laughter and fit perfectly in physical art. Any movement is considered physical art.

Examples
Physical art motivates a person to keep moving towards their goals. For example, the future, 2020 World Olympics is in the making. It can be considered as community art because multiple people are coming together

to make it a memorable experience. Physical art is a short and a long term goal during the person's life. In order to make physical art continue, they must practice, such as in the Olympics the Olympians win by doing excessive amounts of practice. This is an example of art, and foremost, art is the expression of human creativity skills and imagination. Art can be found everywhere in our day to day life. Some examples of places are beaches, churches, schools, parks, dancing studios, libraries, work offices, malls, villages, fashion shows, movies, courts, construction sites, parties and etc.

Secondly;

Fashion and physical art inspire me to be a better me and to meet new people. Fashion gives me the gate way to express my thoughts and feelings. Fashion is a way of art because it expresses not only my style but also my personality. I use colorful clothing to express my mood on a daily basis.

Third:

Another art that inspires me is school. School is known for being a community and intellectual art. In school you find a variety of different people from different countries with different backgrounds and cultures. For example,

Antiguans, Jamaicans or Guyanese and so on, once everyone are together we build the schools value. Also we gain communication skills through intellectual art in schools. For example, emailing, music, poems, short stories, books etc.

Art is indeed everywhere as a whole through many factors. When the sky opens up to pour rain, we look and enjoy the view. The food we eat and even the clothes we put in our backs are a form of art. They all consist of color schemes and styles that only artistic people can come up with. To truly understand how art inspired me in the course was physical.

When someone does not have wide range of thinking, they may never see things beyond what they truly can be. The type of art that inspires me is fact it's dealing with just animate objects. You actually have to put in the work to get it done.

This can range from Picasso a statue and even an electronically formed piece. Intellectual art inspired me since it has been able to get my mind going deeper and deeper into thinking process. It has taught me how to open up my mind and think about the things I like but just in an artist's form.

Furthermore, I'm very much inspired by 3-Dimensional Art because it is amazing to me how much a person can bring paintings and drawings to life; they can take you back to past experiences or capture you in the moment with their artwork. All takes a creative and open minded artist to create this type of art.

A person that has inspired and introduced me to get into three dimension or painting and drawing would be this artist named. Example: -"Tracy Lee Stump "she is outstanding artist that has been painting for over Ten years. Mrs. Lee has made lots of people happy because of her works. I am currently study animation art because that is also one of my favorites types of art however I hope that one day I can be just as good as Mrs. Lee.

Art is an inescapable phenomenon that is represented all throughout life, whether it's visual, mental, or even physical; everything carries out its own art form. Art is basically a term used for channeling the creative aspects of all existing things.

I like to think of art as a large segment of life, for it exists in all things. With its six distinctive forms in which it can be embodies most? If we're honest, there is no one answer. It intriguing, because we are people perceives it differently.

Art is everywhere. Which means art is literally all around you. In this book learning anew that art was all around us. I found that extremely fascinating, because that turn me into it, and I am an artist and more, the human share learn and disrepute the art

Leonardo DaVinci:
Leonardo DaVinci was one of renaissance major artist beside Michael Angelo and Raphael. Three major artists, three major types of arts: architecture, sculpture, painting, including the three major towns Vines, Florence, and Rome.

Renaissance is an important part of the history of art. Also, I learned about some of the most important artists in the world, such as Michael Angelo, Leonardo DaVinci, and more. The art that inspires me the most is natural. Natural art is so inspiring because you get to hear and feel the nature that God has given us. Whenever I see lightning bolts, I like to take pictures of them because the shape that they create is amazing and also how the colors contrast with the sky is very interesting to me. I remember when I was younger I used to be amazed at how a crowd of birds in the sky could make the shape when flying in flock.

When I went to Niagara Falls, I was very amazed at how it was interesting and beautiful to look at the creation of God and how art is involved in it. Now whenever I blend three different items in a blender I stare at it and see how all the colors start mixing up together and make one solid color. I consider myself an artist because I really like fashion and sports.

I consider soccer a part of art because when I kick the ball I can make an arc or make the ball go in a curved way and shapes are also a part of today's art. Also, the shape of the ball, the way the field is made and the way the players position to play a game, is another way to express art. Also, whenever I dress, I like to make sure that my outfit is matching because I like to stay in style.

- Technology:

Technology arts are greatly influencing the development of contemporary arts with the introduction of new, more attractive and tougher materials that artists use to create their work.

These innovations have increased the horizons of creativity and opened new artistic frontiers. They have also helped to reduce the amount of time spent in the actual execution of an art piece.

Since the Seventeenth Century, technology has been rapidly growing to the point that is has impacted every characteristic of our lives including art.

Technological arts are used in Cinemas, television, computers, telecom, telephones, tablets, cars building, and houses.

Technology: Technology started from the Seventeen century, the time electricity was invented, from Camera Aboscra. Into different generation, cinema and cinema zoography, television, video, computer laptop, iPad, Telecom, home phone, cellphone, until postmodern invention. Technology is distributed in cars, building, theaters and outer space. Technology is making communication and information easier.

Natural art:

Natural art refers to the phenomena of the physical world and to the life in general. Nature is both around us and deep within us; our bodies, lives and minds depend on the air we breathe and the food we eat, that is why every aspect of our environment is considered natural art: flowers, trees, weather, animals, sky, ground, water, mountains, humans, food, fire, ground, birth, hills, landscape, and oceans, everything around us.

Natural art: - natural art includes: space in the sky, ground and underground. Nature, land, rivers, oceans, lakes, sky ground, earth, rainforest jungle, weather, trees, hills, mountains, landscape, seascape, sand, sandy stone, humans, and animals including food.

How can all these be examples of arts? All of them sharing and including elements and principles of art. What are the elements and the principle of art? You need to think for an idea to do any type of art. Space

materials shape to form and design our need at the moment. Time and motion and all type of art contain value and light line volume. But while practicing need to balance or not (symmetrical or asymmetrical) proportion and scale colored and what attractive and not, subordination invoices, texture smooth rhythm. All elements and principles of art are being founded in the six type of art.
Do you practice all of them every day, Part of them, or at least one of them? What parts are you into? Ask yourself these questions, and you'll realize that you are an artist.

Examples

Art is very important especially when listening to music as intellectual art; Rainbow is a very important art in nature because it forms an art with different colors by the reflection of the sun and water together. Nature is very important in art because you can see it everywhere. Animals are also art because sometimes dogs, cows, cats, and even horse have little color patches on their bodies.

When you see a tornado you can see the shape of it and the art that is being created by nature. Now that I took this course, I strongly believe that art is everywhere because with the six types of art that I was taught, I see every little details and pieces of art that each one has or when just starting to drive near mountains, buildings, houses, and or any three dimension images, etc. especially the way the buildings are made, you could tell an architect is an artist because every time you see different and very beautiful and modern. They bring out new ideas every time and that's an art. From four centuries CE and till today.

Physical and fashion, natural, and technological art. Natural is the art we see daily: clouds, water, trees, and much more. Fashion art is also, daily: Rainbow is a very important art in nature because it forms an arc with different colors by the reflection of the sun and water together. Nature is very important in art because you can see it everywhere. Animals are also art because sometimes dogs, cows, cats, and even horse have little color patches on their bodies. When you se a tornado you can see the shape of it and the art that is being created by nature. Now that I took this course, I strongly believe that art is everywhere because with the six types of art that I was taught, I see every little detail and piece of art that each one has.

The clothes we wear, hair design, wearing makeup is all considered art. The books we read are intellectual art. Computers and internet is technology art. You can also find physical art in everyday walking, running, and jumping, using technology in a Gum. So, you can stop to appreciate art everywhere you are.

Technology art inspires me most. Learning how much has come from one simple idea has amazed me. With technology also advancing daily it keeps the life with high interest to see what will develop next. Technology is a ground-breaking art in history that the world depends on, and uses on a constant daily basis.

Through this book, I discovered some interesting things on how computers have evolved so much since the very first invention (Charles Babbage) made, and through the first computer was basically a calculator it gave the idea to what has been developed today. Engineers and scientists come with more advanced idea year after year. It has been lead us into this world that is based on technology and almost all companies or business are becoming more digital. It has been very convenient and made life easier.

Those were just basic reasons as to why everybody is artist, but there is art involved in everything that the human do on a daily basis. When they wake up and soak in the sunlight that is natural art. The breakfast that they eat is natural art. The clothes they dress themselves in, the shoes that have seen so many miles, the car that has traveled to work so many times, it is all art. Natural art has become less of a commonality and more of an affair to witness. I have always enjoyed hiking. The next time I hike, I will look at nature as earth's art.

Everyone is an artist, and art has given me the insight and knowledge I needed to see this. I would strongly recommend this book to those who are invested in the arts and those who haven't found an appreciation for it yet. Overall, the reviewers of this book found it quite enjoyable and enlightening and they give me a newfound respect for natural art.

Even the phone they use, that distracts me from the natural life, the device that they are all irrefutably attached to, it is all art. Art is integrated into our daily lives; we've come so accustomed to its beauty that most of us don't notice. This is because for so many, art has a simple and definitive value. It's a technology electronic and electric that give us the beauty which envelopes our lives.

The daily experience art, from the choice of clothing to the placement of furniture uniquely design. This art has inspired me to learn more about its value and has given me the desire to explore and appreciate art in its beauty.

Part (3)
Elements and principle of Art

Introduction to the elements of Art

How to present or write about art? For sure you can, but how? Read the following. Art is everywhere from how you style your hair to the nail paint you put on your feet.

If anyone needs to design or create art, what does he need to start? First of all, the idea of what is the meaning and uses; so the idea is first, then the materials, space, shape to form the subject for the idea to become true.

Space to practice is important and to design papers and pencils, shade and light are used to form up the drawing, and colors. The value is important to think about commercial and volume mass and trading.

The elements of Art are;

- Idea; An idea needed to create a house, airplane, painting, drawing, dressing, film, cellphone, hair design, field, shirt, food, book.

-Design; for every image, on space, ground or on our body.

- Materials; Material changes the idea to touchable and real object.

-Time; time to set think and create.

- Space; space occupied by art volume

- Shape; Changing from design and just idea to form.

- Form; buildup

- Light; to see and to figure out
  The tones of the shade and light.

- Line; to follow up the design, different type of line needed; dark line, light, curve, zigzag, vertical, horizontal, diagonal, implied, dancing line, sharp.

- Colors; Warm and cool. Primary, secondary and intermediate from dark to light.

- Textures; the surface is not smooth, different feeling

- Smoothness; not texture.

- Value; There is income value money or could an idea.

- Mass; the weight of the materials or thought
- Volume; space occupied by the object.
- Research; study and get more information to build up the idea or the value
- Changing; important for new design to match the time and need
-sharing; to look for diverse and differentiation.
The element is the beginning and it is a language of art.

The principles of Art

Principles are rules of arts because the human uses it while practicing, researching, adding or subtracting and or to make other changes.

What is the principle of art?

-Material place and time

-Balance; Symmetrical or Asymmetrical balance or mixed;

A- Symmetrical; when the right side is the same left Side

B-Asymmetrical; when the right side is not the same Left side

C-Mixed; part of the design symmetrical other part is not

- Unity; is the mood or the color seems from the same family, cools or warm

- Variety: the mood and the color is not in harmony from the same family looks contrast

- Proportion; is part of the all, like the hanger to the pin or the hand to the body.
- Scale; to compare two different images, a rule to the pencil, or my high to yours.
- Emphases; The attractive area, like the object on the still life, or the vocal point, the main character.
-Subordination; Not attractive which is the area around the object on the still life, or the backyard in the house. The people around the main character.
-Texture; qualities of the Surfaces; not smooth
-Smoothness; flatness not texture sleekness. Like; print paper, wall, drawing, glass.
 - Light; to show the colors
- Line; A thin trace, from dark to light, link or contour line, stripe.
- Rhythm; Time count by drum music, sequence.
- Mood; feeling of the practice moment, attitude.

- Research; Differs Knowledge and citation

-Sharing the idea, participation, contribution.

- changing direction.

-Manuals; created by hand, instruction.

-Technology; power from electric and the movement of postmodern equipment

- Individual or community; Art could be produce by one person, company or group of people. Apply the elements and principles of Art on the six types of arts.

Part (4)
History of Art
And plastic term

History of plastic and plastic Age

Introduction:

The easy way to know about art history is the timeline that comes from Pre-history to Cave age,

Stone Age and middle age, each part divided into three: early, middle, and late. For example: early, middle, and late Stone Age.

The beginning of civilization was important, because it started with gathering near the rivers on purpose of family and protection. The useful of fresh water for; irrigation, drinking, for human, animals, plantation, the easy food (fishing), and transportation.

Most importantly its clay, when they cooked the clay it turns into hard strong body. So the Beginning of civilization was near the River not near the Ocean, and near the Ocean is sandy not muddy like the Rivers.

In terms of the society the population increase and they start to establish law. Stablishing law is the second step inside protection.

The first one against the outsider enemy, animals or natural movement this why the human gather together, the second from the inner movement so the problem coming between them this why the human stablish the law to protect themselves from each other.

As example is Hammurabi's law in Mesopatomun (land the land between two Rivers): tigress and AL - frat which is Iraq today. The beginning is a spotlight of Human development.

Stone Age is part of classic area, which is Pre-history, cave age, Stone Age and middle age. Can we add the plastic age, if we jump from classic era to modern era?

What is plastic Age?

- It's A Plastic world

1284

Plastic was invented around 1284, the first plastic creations being a horn and a tortoiseshell. In 1823, Macintosh discovered rubber. In 1845, inventor Bewley found a way to produce natural rubber from a plant called gutta percha; this plant rapidly gained fame in the 19th century.

1862

Londoner Alexander Parker revealed the first manmade plastic compound in 1862, but it didn't succeed due to the high cost. Inventor John W. Hyatt invented Celluloid, which is considered to be the first thermoplastic.

1897

In 1897, two German researchers studied different types of plastic that is still used today (buttons). In 1920 Coco Channel introduced jewelry made from Bakelite (plastic).

1931

In 1931, a strong and transparent type of plastic called Plexiglas was created in two different laboratories. Chemist Stephanie Kwolek developed a resistant plastic known and used by military and police in bullet resistive protective wear today.

The first truly synthetic plastic was invented by Leo Baekeland, a Belgium chemist who lived in New York. In 1905, he found out that when he combined formaldehyde and phenol, he produced a material that bound all types of powders. It was the first thermosetting plastic in the world. This was a material that, once hardened, would not soften under heat.

1932-1933-1934

This material had so many uses it was called "the material of different uses." The invention of plastic inspired many new variations of plastic such as neoprene in 1932, polythene in 1933 and Perspex in 1934.

Many people use plastic to make bags or water bottles. Plastic is being used to keep food fresh and homely. Everything that people buy in the supermarkets is wrapped in plastic.

Plastic is even used in the making of automobiles. Some cars have plastic bumpers installed. They are very useful because if you are in a collision it will lessen the amount of damage done to the car.

The plastic is easy to switch, or the old one can be used effectively. With low friction, high strength and naturally smooth finish, acetyl is an ideal material to use such as in a steering column switch. There are many different uses for plastic in cars and they all add to the performance of cars.

The versatility of plastic materials comes from the ability to mold, laminate, shape, and tailor them physically and chemically. There is a plastic suitable for almost any application.

Plastic; Origins and importance

Plastic is a word that originally means "pliable and easily shaped." It only recently became a name for a category of material called polymers. The word polymers mean "of many parts," Polymers are made of long chains of molecules. Cellulose, the material that makes the cell wall of plants, is a very common natural polymer.

Over the last century and a half, humans have learned how to make synthetic polymers, sometimes using natural substances arranged in repeating units often much longer than those found in nature. It is the length of these chains and the patterns in which they are arrayed that make polymers strong, lightweight, and flexible. In other word it's what makes them so plastic. These properties make synthetic polymers exceptionally useful, and since we learned how to create and manipulate them, polymers have become as essential part of our lives. Over the last 50 years, plastics have saturated our world and changed the way that we live. The first plastic based on a synthetic polymer was made from phenol and formaldehyde, with the first viable and cheap synthesis method invented in 1907, by Leo Hendrik Baekeland.

Plastic is a material we use on a day to day bases but never put much thought into how it was created. Around the early 1900s, Bakelite was reported by a Belgian chemist named Leo Baekeland in a using phenol and formaldehyde substance. Right after world War l, there was an improvement in chemical technology which led to an expansion in types of plastics, with mass product beginning around the 1940s and 1950s.

Among the earliest examples in the wave polymers were polystyrene, which was originally produced by BASF in the 30's and polyvinyl chloride. Plastic is a recyclable material that can be reused so we should take advantage of how this material can be utilized for the greater good of modern civilization. With the creation of new and different types of plastic emerged a wave of new ways to use items in our day to day lives.

In our uses of plastic there are tons and tons of ways we use it as a necessity in our daily lives. I consistently use plastic in my life. For example, I use plastic in my glasses frame. It's a lot cheaper and has lasted me almost 2 years with little to no scratches or damage done to them.

I also use plastic to hold my frozen food in, plastic is very easily manipulated and can form into virtually anything, so being an air locked bag to preserve food is just one of the wonders of plastic. We also can use plastic for our cellular devices, almost all house phones being used out of types of plastic which is durable and can last you more than 10 years. Plastic honestly makes our lives so much simpler but what it helps us with can also be its worse aspect.

Since plastic is a disposable it is actually contaminating the earth. Much of our marine life has been affected by the discarded plastic because people don't recycle plastic or think it can do damage to anyone or thing. Even though plastic has made our lives as humans better, we haven't put much thought into what it does to the animals that also inhabit our world.

Importance and useful of plastic
Yes, plastic is a very beneficial material to our society and has helped move us forward in art, technology and so much more. We should appreciate all the good we have done with plastic but also realize that plastic does not have it is bad factors. We need to work in recycling and reusing our plastic items.

In today's day in age we use plastic in our everyday lives without second thought of what we are using. Plastic can be mass produced in a fraction of the time that other materials can be shaped or molded to be used. But with all the adventures that having plastic around there are so many disadvantages and cons that plastic has on the environment and us. Even though we use plastic for amazing things it still can harm us and harm our future. Plastic is in almost everything we use from television's to sneakers, plastic has taken over our lives. We even use plastic to hold and help preserve our food but do we put that much thought into what happens after we have finished using it?

Plastic has been a very helpful material to us humans but more harmful than helpful to the animals. We use plastic as in six packs of canned drinks to old them together, the item holding them together is made of plastic and is supposed to be cut open and then discarded but many people don't and because of this you see a lot of sea animals swimming with these alien object around their necks or body disfiguring them. Some of our plastic waste can even be mistaken for food by wild life and kill them. Most of the garbage made of plastic that is left in the streets can be swooped up by a bird and kill them because it's toxic to ingest plastic for small animals.

The things we use don't only affect us humans, but also the animals around us. We are sharing this planet so we have to stay accountable for all the wrong things we do to it by ignoring how we dispose of our garbage.

Even though plastic isn't usually very damaging or dangerous to us humans but not only can it affect us but also our air is affected by the manufacturing of plastics, this is because as it is being made it releases toxic chemicals into the air. Chemicals like carcinogenic, neurotoxic, and hormone destructive chemicals are normally used in the creation of plastic products, these chemicals being released into the air may not seem like a big deal but over years and years of having it put into the air it has helped cause pollution.

A lot of the chemicals put into plastic are the most damaging chemicals you can use and due to its years of distribution has created high levels of toxicity in the air. This amount of toxic air cannot be helpful for not even our species but all specie.

Plastic affection
How plastic affect the water creature:-
In the ocean, plastic debris injures and kills fish, seabirds and marine mammals. Marine plastic pollution has impacted at least 267 species worldwide, including 86% of all sea turtle species, 44% of all seabirds and 43% of all marine mammal species.

The impacts include fatalities as a result of ingestion, starvation, suffocation, infection, drowning, and entanglement, (Clean Water Action) Most of the marine trash and debris comes from land-based sources. Food containers, food packaging and plastic bags are the largest component of the waste in the ocean.

Many sea turtles die from plastic bags are the largest component of the waste in the ocean. Many sea turtles die from plastic because they look very similar to jellyfish. The plastics get trapped in their stomach, which prevents them from properly swallowing food. Plastic debris, laced with chemicals and often ingested by marine animals, can injure or poison wildlife. (Knoblauch)

Marine debris is mostly made up of plastic. We have over 5.25 trillion particles of plastic in our oceans. Marine animals suffer tremendously from our increased consumption of non-biodegradable plastic. Around the world, an estimated 100,000 marine mammals and sea turtles die each year when they become trapped in plastic or eat it, perhaps mistaking it for food. More than half of sea turtles have eaten plastic.

Even on the land, or agricultural the animals in danger; if any animals eat part of the plastic, the plastic materials not digested, and will not come out of the stomach, and that cost deices get to death, in human stomach cost cancer and death too.

The plastics industry, through the leadership of the American Chemical Council (ACC), spends millions of dollars each year to convince policy makers and Californians that solutions to plastic pollution lie in anti-litter campaigns that attribute the responsibility for marine debris on individual behavior. Yet they have devoted little funding to public education and much more on promoting policies that support increased use of plastics. (Clean Water Action)

Items like plastic bags when they break down, they readily soak up and release toxins that can contaminate soil and water, and harm the Fish, animals and spread into groundwater.

Plastic buried deep in landfills can leach harmful chemicals that spread into ground water (Knoblauch) It is not just the accumulation of plastic that harms the environment, but it also the fragments and toxins released during decomposition that pollute our soil and water.

Certain plastics are designed to degrade even though they become less noticeable they are still present and harmful to the environment.

I am trying to reduce the use of plastic because it is useful but the overproduction is harming the environment. I do think that plastic is useful but the overproduction is harming the environment. I do think that plastic is useful but the overproduction is harming the environment.

I don't like the fact that many marine animals die from plastic, it is not their fault that the plastic looks like food to them. The amount of plastic pollution in the ocean and how many marine animals it kills within the year is an outstanding number. It is unreal to think that we are killing all these poor innocent sea creatures. Why not in country or some part of country avoid using plastic?

California has banned the use of plastic bags in 2014. It is good to know that they care about their environment and sea animals.

An example would be certain ocean environments the plastic fragments are taken in by filter feeding organisms, even though certain plastic are designed to degrade quickly. Floating plastic waste that can survive thousands of years in water can serve as a transportation device for invasive species that disrupt habitats. (Bio-Tec) Since certain plastic release harmful toxins it can be dangerous to human health.

A lot of plastic already contains toxins, such as phthalates, BPA and flame retardants. And as plastic breaks down, it can absorb many dangerous toxins more easily, such as damaging pesticides like DDT, PCB and PAH. (Creeks Life). People are exposed to these chemicals not only during manufacturing, but also by some plastic packaging.

Some of the plastic packaging to the foods is dangerous because contain part of the plastic. Examples of plastics contaminating food have been reported with most plastic types including Styrene from polystyrene, plasticizers from PVC, antioxidants from polyethylene, and Acetaldehyde from PET. (Ecology Center)

People are exposed to chemicals from plastic multiple times per day through the air, dust, water, food and use of consumer products. Polyvinyl Chloride (PVC) is commonly used in food packaging, containers for toiletries, floor tiles, shower curtains etc. This type of plastic can cause cancers, birth defects, ulcers, skin disease, genital changes, etc.

Polyethylene (PET) is found in water and soda bottles, chewing gum, drinking glasses, food containers, plastic bags, toys, etc. This type of plastic is suspected human carcinogen (substance capable of causing cancer in living tissue). There are eight more plastics that are harmful to human health. It is hard to avoid plastic because we live in a world surrounded by plastic. We are in a real plastic age.

How to support the environment:-
The human will get a lot of devotion and fund much more on promoting and supporting the use of plastics. While educating the young to prevent littering, the proper management of litter fails to address the unsustainable consumption of resources involved in producing packaging and the use of easy packed good like plastic water bottles. As the amount of disposable packaging and products continues to increase, controlling litter through public education and cleanup of streets and waterways requires significant and sustained funding.

Reduces the use of plastic and recycle. Everybody can help save the environment by keeping plastic The chemical use in the creating of plastic is very harmful for the human body and not only humans but also for animals and our environment.

Thanks to the cheap material of plastic hundreds of people use bottles, cans more than 5 million pieces of plastic consumed each year. And our oceans and sea get destroyed but plastic and the creatures that live in them get injured or die thanks to it. Out of the landfills, air, and oceans as well as cut down on natural resources use to make new plastics. We can try and reduce the use of plastic, by using reusable bags instead of plastic bags. Recycle plastic to reduce the pollution in the ocean and environment.

Suggestions on how to avoid plastic products whenever possible buy food in glass or metal containers, avoid heating food in plastic containers, or storing food in plastic containers. This will help reduce the risk of disease that most plastic toxins give to humans.

Industry food and Plastic

The material of a different uses for example: plastic surgery. Plastic is also used in the human body to change faces and body parts. This is very risky. From the 20th century through now plastic has been used almost on everything even on the human body. Plastic is a very reusable item. It's what we humans use to make money and to make our "lives better".

Plastic is not always good, it has left harmful imprints on the environment and human. If plastic is not recycled it can end up in the ocean and many marine animals either eat or get caught in plastic. That's why we need to be very cautious about the way we use plastic.

Plastic has left harmful imprints on the environment. Items like plastic bags or bottle are thrown away every day, and end up in trash sites. They can also end up in forests, creeks, rivers, seas and oceans all around the world. That is because some people loiter and don't realize how useful is can be.

While some of these items are recycled, the growth of plastic consumption is through the roof. Plastic is not biodegradable, but photodegradable. And in reality, most plastic does not ever disappear, but becomes long-lasting 'plastic dust'. (Creek Life)

The bad thing about plastic is that it is harmful to the environment it takes 400 to 1,000 years to disintegrate. It is only one hundred percent recyclable but it is costly to recycle. Many people do recycle plastic in their own way, by reusing plastic products.

There are many people who reuse plastic bags to give someone food or to pick up other materials. People also reuse plastic water bottles, but they are good to read for a couple of times if they are washed properly with hot soapy water. Others buy plastic containers. This helps the food stay fresh and makes it convenient for people to take food anywhere they want.

Plastic used for the storage of food. Once people walk into the supermarket there is bread wrapped in plastic for freshness. Then, you walk down the fruit and vegetables isle there is plastic tags that tie up vegetables.

While shopping down the fruit and vegetable it is automatic to grab plastic bags for fruit. It is something that people have been accustomed to and do not even second guess how important plastic is to us. They protein products in the supermarket are also wrapped in plastic for freshness, been usually come in a plastic bag and wrapped in saran wrap. It helps the food stay fresh longer and makes it easier for people to buy food.

The use of plastic in third world countries contributes to the mass pollution that has been building up in the last 50 years. A lot of third world countries do not properly discard their plastic waste which leaves toxic and hazardous matter out that can cause damage to the plant life in the area.

The lack of properly recycled plastic can not only disturb our ecosystem but hurt us as individuals. Without plastic being recycled it is so much harder to grow crops and get fresh clean water, were as people living in these underdeveloped countries live off the produce they generate from their communities. With this

Lack of food generating in the community it not only can cause starvation but hurts our ozone layer because of the toxic fumes created by plastic.

Plastic has helped our society create everyday objects faster and more effectively, but with its advantages it also has its disadvantages. This material that has come to play a big role in our day to day lives is actually very harmful to the world around us. A serious question should be, is it better to have a world with plastic where it helps destroy our ecosystem or a world without plastic and less advantages in medical equipment, food storage, and even our shoes.

Our society uses plastic so much we usually don't even look into how harmful it is to us. Also, the harmful effects of plastic on aquatic life are devastating, and accelerating.

In addition to suffocation, ingested, and other macro-particulate causes of death in larger birds, fish, and mammals, the plastic in ingested by smaller and smaller creatures (as it breaks down into smaller and smaller particles) and bio-accumulates in greater and greater concentrations up the food chain—with humans at the top. Exacerbating these problems of persistence and bioaccumulation is plastic's propensity to act as a magnet and sponge for persistent organic pollutants such as polychlorinated biphenyls (PCBs) and thee pesticide DDT.

So, in addition to ingesting the physically and chemically damaging plastic compounds, aquatic life is also ingesting concentrated quantities of highly bio-accumulative compounds that are some of the most potent toxins found on the planet. Again, this bioaccumulation increase in concentration as it works up the food chain and into our diets.

Toxic chemical release during manufacture is another significant source of the negative environmental impact of plastics. A whole host of carcinogenic, neurotoxic, and hormone-disruptive chemicals are standard ingredients and waste products of plastic production, and they inevitably find their way into our ecology through water, land, and air pollution. Some of the more familiar compounds include vinyl chloride (in PVC and others), formaldehyde, and bisphenol-A, or BPA (in polycarbonate).

Many of these are persistent organic pollutants (POPs)-some of the most damaging toxins on the planet, owing to a combination of their persistence in the environment and their high levels of toxicity.

The versatility of plastic materials comes from the ability to mold, laminate or shape them, and to tailor them physically and chemically. There is a plastic suitable for almost any application.

Plastic is harmful to the environment; the decomposing process of plastic product can last from 400 to 1000 Years with newer 'degradable" compound. Since the degradation process is slow the waste plastic will clog our waterways, ocean, forest, and other natural habits that are filled with animals who mistake dangerous plastic for food. Chemical dangerous are also high, because both creation and recycling of plastic produce toxic materials of many kinds.

Plastic produce toxic fumes when it is burnt and it is harmful to humans and the environment. The production of plastic has grown over the last 50 Years. This is a reason why we live in the plastic age, plastic is all around us. It may sound funny but we wear plastic every day. It is on our clothing and in our hair and shoes. It is even with the food we buy plastic protects the food from spoiling.

This affects humans in many ways; we no longer know what life is without plastic because it is used daily. It affects the way we live and how we view the world. It is interesting how much we use plastic and don't even realize. We have grown accustomed to plastic being all around us; people have forgotten what life is like without plastic.

During the grave-phase of plastics; the disposal phase, Natural organisms have a very difficult time breaking down the tremendous problem of the material's persistence. A very small amount of total plastic production (less than 100%) is effectively in limbo for hundreds of thousands of years, or to be accumulated in biotic forms throughout the surrounding ecosystem.

Plastics have low density and thus if frequently migrates "downstream," blowing out of landfills and off garbage barges. For decades marine biologist and researchers had been witnessing increasing amounts of plastic garbage contamination in the ocean.

1997
Then, in 1997, as mentioned in the introduction, Captain Charles Moore discovered widespread plastic garbage contamination in an area larger than the state of Texas that had formed within a cyclonic region, called a gyre, in the North Pacific Ocean.

2005
By 2005, the estimated area of contamination expanded to 10 million square miles, nearly the size of Africa. Ninety percent of this garbage was

determined to be plastic, and 80% was originally sourced from land, such as construction waste so Captain Moore found where "downstream" goes. Early sampling determined approximately 3 million tons of plastic on the surface; the United Nations Environment Program reports that 70% of marine refuse sinks below the surface, which would suggest a staggering 100 million of plastic in this one area of the Pacific alone with more entering every day. There are six similar gyres across the planet's oceans, each laden with plastic refuse (Weisman 2007).

Plastic in the Home:
There is a huge percentage of plastic in our television, our sound system, our cell phone, our vacuum cleaner- and probably plastic foam in our furniture too.
Our floor covering if it is not real wood probably has a synthetic/natural fiber blend (just like some of the clothes you wear).

We have plastic chair or bar stool seats, plastic countertops (acrylic composites, plastic linings (PTFE) in our non-stick cooking pans, plastic plumbing in our water system- the list is almost endless.

Industry Plastic in the food:
Often times, we wrap our food in PVC cling film before preserving it in the refrigerator, yogurt in plastic tubs, cheese in plastic wrap and water and milk in blow-molded plastic containers. There are plastics which now prevent gas escaping from pressurized soda bottles, but cans and glass are still #1 for beer. Although almost all beers car canned, it's interesting to know that the cans are lined with plastic.

Plastics in Transport:
Trains, airplanes, and automobiles-even ships, satellites and space stations all use plastics extensively. In every mode of transport, plastic is used extensively, for example:
- seating
- Paneling
- Instrument enclosure
- Surface covering
Plastics are even used in combination with other materials as structural elements in all kinds of transport. Yes,

even skateboards, roller blades and bicycles.

Without plastics many possessions that we take for granted might be out of reach for all but the richest Americans, Replacing natural materials with plastic has made many of our possessions cheaper, lighter, softer and stronger.

Plastics are a part of our daily lives. Unfortunately, that doesn't mean they're safe or responsible. A closer understanding of the harmful effects of plastic will empower us to improve their toxic footprint.

In conclusion; we can observe by the plastic timeline that it has been very helpful and successful such as the creation of plastic jewelry and buttons for our clothes. And now-a-days computers, phones, tablets, calculators, notebooks, pens, and many other things are quite useful too. But, throughout time it has become very harmful for us and our environment such as forests, oceans, and our seas land creatures also are affected by it.

Have you ever started drinking a bottle of water and looked at the bottle and think to yourself "plastic bottles are such a handy invention, how did they come about?" Well plastic is a polymer based matter with a long repetition of carbon molecules. Polymer's placidity is what allows the carbon molecules to take any shape the creator chooses such a bottle shape.

1907
Plastic was officially introduces into our society around 1907 by a man Leo Baekeland. Although there are many cases of scientists tracing plastics back into the early 1800's.

1930-1935
moving a little bit further into history around 1930 is when synthetic plastics was founded by also by Baekeland including polystyrene in 1929, polyester in 1930,

polyvinylchloride (PVC) and polythene in 1933, nylon in 1935. These new findings brought into an era we are still currently in which is becoming a bit of a scare to the ecosystem called the Plastic era.

1948

Although plastic is starting to become a problem for our ecosystem since it's not biodegradable, it still has many useful qualities. One of the biggest inventions that came from plastic is everyday house hold Tupperware which was invented in 1948.

Before the inventing of Tupperware there was no such things as "leftovers" when it came cooked food. If left out overnight food would spoil, but thanks to plastic people saved a good chunk of change on being able to save the surplus of food. Another big creation from plastic came plastic bottles and canteens allowing the average person to travel and carry a sufficient water supply with them. These were a big hit for the military since metal canteens were causing unknowing sickness to the soldiers drinking from them.

Although plastic has found its ways to win our hearts, plastic is slowly taking over our planet. Since plastic isn't biodegradable it makes it harder to find a place to put all of this plastic. Even when attempted to be burned, or crushed tiny particles break off and eventually make their ways back to our oceans through the water cycle.

Henderson Island is a small island in the Pacific Ocean and it's estimated to be home to over 38 million pieces of plastic and counting. This is a danger to animals and humans since micro bacteria builds up into the plastic and starts to pollute the water it floats in.

In conclusion, humans are to have a very love hate relationship with plastic.

The good for now is out weighing the bad, we have much more use for plastic then we can afford to not use it. With this being said all hope is not lost, scientist is working on a biodegradable plastic made of corn starch. They hope to have all of the kinks worked out a few years down the road. Mother earth has a long, fruitful, and hopefully plastic free life ahead of it.

Part (5)

Art criticism

Art criticism
Literature, Poem and picture
(Visual and intellectual)
What to do in the Museum

It is not enough to practice art better to judge the art.
- Art criticism, Critical Thinking about intellectual (Story poems) or two dimension art (Picture). From eight to fifteen steps for art's judgment.

1-*Information;
Could be about picture, building, book, shirt, shoes, furniture, park or school. Information is five.
A-The title
B-The name of the creator, Artist or engineer
C-The material
D- The size
E-The date
2-Description;
To describe means just count and list whatever you see, or figure out,

images space color, lines without judge. Using line to divide the artwork helper judging the artwork, horizontal or vertical lines partition helps to break down the image.

3-Analysis;

How the creator organizes the artwork important to know the direction, horizontal line and the partitions if they looks in the same or differs, more the center. What comes first and second, the art analysis, the artist theory to organize.

4-Interpretation;

The artist idea, start with who, what is he want to do and why. The artist idea about the art could be from three to five paragraphs. Make sure not your idea, the artist idea.

5-Judgment;

Your own idea, her different circle could be used; social life, beauty, political, commercial, religious, personal.

6-Formal theory;

Is what type of art, realistic, imagination, impression, abstract, cubism, romantic, romanticism, classic or classicism, surrealism?

7-Social cultural theory; to answer the question, this art from where? Which continent, country, location, tribe or family.

8-Expressive;

Come out with new idea.

9-Biography (of the creator)

The background and resume with a reference.

Conclusion

(One paragraph about one point from, 1 to 9)

10-*Ask questions to yourself

1-Do you draw a picture in your mind about the artwork

A-Visualize the characters (The image, human, animals or nature)

B-Connect the Art to the (place and time)

C-Relate the subject to the (past, present and the future)

1-D-on conclusion write one

paragraph from one point, A to C)

2-*Do you like the artwork? Why.

3-Which part does you like or dislike, (compare and contrast).

4-Can you explain, describe give example remind you what?

5-Go back to the title or the introduction takes a moment and listens to yourself.

6-Conclusion

(One paragraph about one point from. 12 to 15)

3-*Tied up brake down subject into three parts.

A-General; include the topic and statement

B-Topic: part of the general idea connected general and statement but it is not stated.

C-Statement should be specific and short, end into the title of the subject.

Intellectual

Al-Biraiyab's Story

Art criticism about Al-Biraiyab's story and Poem about Al-Biraiyab?

Example 1; intellectual--Example and practice; Al-Biraiyab's Story;

Al-Biraiyab

Al-Biraiyab is not a village. It is a group of domes in a thick forest with a lot of movements be around it. Islamic scholars were buried under these domes, which changed into shrines and graves where visitors, shepherds, and some dervishes roam this forest.

These domes were anciently built between Fangol and Wedi (small valley) Al-Qubah (dome). They were built for the three sons of Bari: Dafallah, Ali, and Bazbar. They were religious sheikhs and scholars. It is said that they came from Rubatab region and settled in this valley, opened Al-Khalawi (native religious schools) to memorize Holy Quran and learn Arabic. They taught people religious matters and as a result the region is named after them. That was before the British invasion.

Al-Biraiyab became famous and has followers and disciples who gathered around them for different purposes. The British took notice of the gathering around these religious Sheikhs and imposed heavy unbearable taxes on them. The people left their homes, Al-Khalawi, region, and dispersed in different parts of Sudan.

Some of the people lived in Omdurman and Al-Jazera in Wad Madani regions. Some of them left to western Sudan. Only Faki (religious teacher) Mahmoud Abu Shara, his son Abdulrahman, and some Biraiyab families stayed in the region.

Sayed Bari, former President of Somalia, is from the Biraiyab family. Some natives of the region used to frequent visits to Sayed Bari.

Origins of many rulers of neighboring countries are traced back into the Sudan e.g. the mother of sister Egypt's President Mohammed Najeeb is from Wad Madani region, the mother of President Anwar Al-Sadat of Egypt is also from Omdurman, President Eidi Amin of Uganda is from the tribes of Southern Sudan, and President Idris Dibe of Chad is from Darfur.

Al-Komur region has absorbed the religious spirit that goes back to Biraiyab and Sufi education. It taught people how to face life with the least and death with eyes of faith. They took from it the wisdom of asceticism and austerity that shrouds the Sufi life in Sudan. They receive the new born baby with voicing the calling to prayer in his ears and farewell their dead chanting:

"I conclude my utterance with prayers upon Prophet (PBUH). Oh Allah may you always prey upon and bless Prophet Mohammed, his companions, and forefathers. A prayer that excels musk in glorified fragrance."

They pour down soil on the grave of the deceased and go for their cultivation and picking.

These domes still have reverence in the souls of natives of the region. This awe is stemming from the respect of people to anyone who adheres to beliefs of Islam. The domes became a cemetery with religious tales and surrounded by a thick forest of Laloub, mimosa, and acacia trees called the forest of Awlad (sons of) Bari.

Critical Thinking about the Story

1 -Information;
A-The title: - Al-Biraiyab
B-The name of the creator: The author, Omar M. Saeed
C-The material: Intellectual writing on paper
D- Six papers writing size: 5x8"
E -The Date -2006
2 -Description:
Three domes in a bushy forest with a lot of movements be around it. Islamic scholars were buried under these domes, which changed into shrines and graves. The daily visitor's come to the place of worship and fun.
3-Analysis:
In short story writing; get direct to the point, and how the author analyses the story, the place and the time, the characters., the main idea, opening, topic and close-up.
4 -Interpretation:
Describe the society and place
North of Sudan, happiness and Sadness.

5 -Judgment:

It is resinous and political story united the community.

6 -Formal theory:

True story

7 -Social cultural theory:

Happen at north east Africa North of Sudan, The Nile River region, Al-Matama distract, Alkomur village.

8 -Expressive:

The story travel to different area in Sudan because the colonist inforce Al-biraiyb to move out the region, as family they scattered not only but as Idea.

9 -Biography (of the creator): The backgrounder author: The author is from the same area. He is a teacher author, artist, and poetry. Born at Al-Komur village at 1953

10 - Conclusion

(One paragraph about one point from, (1 to 9)

The story describes a place combine African and Arabic. The worship is Islamic, the dome located between the Nile River and the mountain, the nature represent African and Arabia, desert and Nile. So the nature and races supplies the habit of the people. On nineteen century British occupied Sudan and the power of the colonist come through the human to control them.

11 -Ask questions to yourself

A-Do you draw a picture in your mind?

B-Visualize the characters, place and time) Nineteen century

C-Connect what you see or read

to the human, animals or nature

to represent Desert and Nile.

D- Relate the subject to the past, present and the future.

Exist as postmodern event.

E-Conclusion (one paragraph about one point from, (A to E)

The story is small scale pictured the big frame of the sofi in Sudan. This frame involved political and social life to be part of sofi life. The entertainment and happiness in midge activates is the other side of the religion. Al people connected from their heart to the area.

12- *Do you like the artwork? Why.

13- Which part you like or dislike, compare and contrast.

14- Can you explain, describe give example remind you what?

15- Go back to the title or the introduction takes a moment listen to you.

16 -Conclusion (one paragraph about one point from. (12 to 15)

17-Tied up brake down subject into three parts.

A-General

B-Topic

C-Statement should be specific and short. It is the title of the subject,

I like the story because about Human nature and social life, and remind me my childhood, the topic is the area religion and the happiness. Al-biraiyb is and a family teaches the people to live a simple life and to share the small thing they have, the reason why the area and the people under Al-Biraiyab's name.

Poem
Shashay Tran's plant

*   *   *

I call shashayTrans plant
Near the river hit by waves near and
far
Between Fangool Sawarid and Say
*   *   *

And Alsada's Mountain, Omzor Hill
In Wad-Bary gone to visit
The sound of our girls who give
money and supplication Oh! We will
not explain and do not ignore
*   *   *

We promise a gift to the father of
Abshara the protector
The one who lives in the hidden
valley
Appear...
Allow me to see clearly
*   *   *

The twin sons of Jabber live
northward
Above the colored hill Pairing in the
night filled with stars

Be Take care of the Nile State and
Sudan
* * *

Our fruitful land
The liquid Gum descends from the
tree
Breaks and mends the tree bark
The plant carries with open flowers
* * *

Alkomur's land that meets the Nile is
patched with green plantation.
The palm branches are covered by
dates and the Dome are scattered on
the ground.
As I speak the beautiful description of
my land with a sweet taste. The
beautiful description of my land is
actually indescribable
* * *

Birds fly closely over the high area of
the Nile
At times flying and other times
landing
The waves hit the ship
The date palm's bark is filled with
water and floating on the Nile.
* * *

The sugar cane is segmented
The corn and birds have wings that
cry
The Aldahaseer plants grow along the
middle of the road
The dew on the grass releases a scent
*   *   *

The waves move the shashay Tran's
plant back and forth
I hope the cold wind wills Carry you
close by
Near or far you remain close by
*   *   *

Why do you constantly come and
leave?
Playing with the geese of the Nile
Every time I hold your branch
You resist
Resistance similar to grabbing water
*   *   *

I can't hold you by hand or by net
The wind will defeat you and bring
you back
I am waiting the Nile wind
To bring me the shashay's branch
*   *   *

From Hobaje and Fangool

From the edge of the Nile,
Sawarid or Say
I am waiting for the Nile wind
To bring me shashy's Trans plant
branch
* * *

Al-Shashai Tran's plant Criticisms

1-Information

    a- title: Al-Shashai Tree
    b- The poetry: The author
    c- Size The: Four pages
    d- Material: writing on papers
    e- Date: 2010

2-Description

The writing translated from Arabic to English divided into four line each. The stars separate each division

3-Analysis

After translation the writing turn to start from left, the line contain two word up to four

4-Interpretation

Al-Shashai Tree metaphor female, from fangole village, the place east of al Komur village among the mountain near the Nile River. The lady not close not too far from her lover, and always the wind carry her far and near and she always the winner. The lover aske the Nile waves to get her near, he wait because he trust the wave and for sure the wave will print hero him.

5-Judgment

It is up to the reader to write what he feels could be at least one paragraph.

6-Formal theory

Realistic

7-Social and cultural theory

From north east Africa location Alkomur region Fangool village

8-Expressive

The poem is excretion of al bareab story and the picture, it is approve the literature (poem and story) and the two dimension is the same) because the elements and the principles of art is the same.

9-Poplougraphy

About the author dedicated teacher, writer, poet and artist

10-History and context

Al-Biraiyab (1882-2016)

Al-Biraiyab is not a village. It is a group of domes in a thick forest with a lot of movements be around it. Islamic scholars were buried under these domes, which changed into shrines and graves where visitors, shepherds, and some dervishes roam this forest.

These domes were anciently built between Fangol and Wedi (small valley) Al-Qubah (dome). They were built for the three sons of Bari: Dafallah, Ali, and Bazbar. They were religious sheikhs and scholars. It is said that they came from Rubatab region and settled in this valley, opened Al-Khalawi (native religious schools) to memorize Holy Quran and learn Arabic. They taught people religious matters and as a result the region is named after them. That was before the British invasion.

Al-Biraiyab became famous and has followers and disciples who gathered around them for different purposes. The British took notice of the gathering around these religious Sheikhs and imposed heavy unbearable taxes on them. The people left their homes, Al-Khalawi, region, and dispersed in different parts of Sudan.

11-Media and processes

Social life and design of dome them.

12-Fundamentals

Location, political, or religion.

13-Themes

The poem is rhythm, movement and mood.

Art criticism about Al-Biraiyab's Painting

(Visual)

- Domes: of Al-Biraiyab
-the Artist: Omar Saeed
-materials: water colors on paper the size: 18"x22"
-The date: 2004
1-*Information
A-The title Al-Biraiyab a group of domes:
B-The name of the Artist: Omar M. Saeed
C-The materials: water color on paper.
D-The size: 18"x22"
E-The date: 2004
2-Description:

Horizontal line sky and ground, sky warm and cool colors, on the ground groups of dome, people and trees.

3-Analysis:

The horizontal line divided the picture into two sky and ground. The sky contains warm and cool dark and light reflect on the ground a domes, human and trees.

4-Interpretation:

The artist draws and paints the land he belong to, because he is away from his home and warm feeling he painted his picture into hot red color. The picture reminds him his childhood, friends and the nature of the region.

5-Judgment:

Your own idea, If the judgment for the audience for long time from 2006 different ideas come around the picture, the visitors male and female many married come from the meeting near the domes, and the people connected the marriage to the bless of the area, for different time they ask and they put some money for blessing to make it fast. In history there is political issue and family life, on vacation and weekend the neighborhood make bareback you for fun and entertainment the area is socialize.

6-Formal theory:

-Realistic

7-Social cultural theory:

Happen at north east Africa North of Sudan, The Nile River region, Al-Matama distract, and Alkomur village.

8-Expressive:

Expressive come from a couple of questions, the education speared out is it the same believe, is the people still the out cook there, how about the technology and communication by cellphone to day. Part of the past is disappearing but still religious and history area.

9-Biography (of the creator) the background

10-Conclusion (one paragraph about one point from, 1 to 9)

11-*Ask questions to yourself

A-Do you draw a picture in your mind?

B-Visualize the characters,(place and time)

C-Connect what you see or read to the human, animals or nature

D- Relate the subject to the past, present or the future.

E-Conclusion (one paragraph the point from, A to E)

12-*Do you like the artwork? Why.

13-Which part you like or dislike, compare and contrast.

14-Explain, describe give example remind you what?

15-Go back to the title or the introduction takes a moment listen to you.

16-Conclusion (one paragraph the point from. 12 to 15)

17-*Tied up; brake down subject into three parts.

A-General

B-Topic

C-Statement should be the title of the subject.

Part (6)

Examples
Desert and Nile

Desert and Nile jock

On 1999 I travel with my family to united states of America, I rented in, Jersey City New Jersey, the tenant is multicultural chines, African, Indian, middle eastern Friend of mine set to gather. I asked the group about doctors for my family.

They said: there are two Egyptian doctors; Doctor Badawe and tomsah (crocodile); I laugh loud and I said to them Desert and Nile.

The group said: what is that? I said Badawen from the desert and Tomsah is from the Nile River; they said; oh that is right, that is right. One from the sand, sand sheikh, other is from the Nile, Nile man!!

Example 1
Desert and Nile

Between reality and Function
**Desert and Nile School of Analysis
and Criticism**
-The Nile
The Nile heads northwards from Khartoum up to Al-Hugnah Village, where the 1st cataract at Jabal (mount) Al-Rawyan not far away from Jabal Al-Atshan. In this place a compass is formed in the nature of land from mountains and cataracts that turned the course of the Nile eastwards.

The compass points east towards Al-Komur village. The Nile's current follows the direction. The compass turned the water current as if the Nile has sprang anew. The current stabs the depth of land and heads eastwards fast and eager to meet the sand of the Desert.

This spring meets another desert spring from the east, from the Empty Quarter in the Arabian Peninsula. Its sands head westwards to enter Sudan and cuddle with the Nile.

The thirst sand waves coming from the east, meet the Nile's flood to irrigate the thirst Desert on the land of cataracts in northern Sudan.

If you pass through the Desert road that divides Al-Komur into two parts, then the scene is pitiful. But the road that goes parallel to the Nile evokes you to feel hopeful. There are green patches, water, sands, and a stroke of soil on the people's bodies.

Earth plates moved deep down the land of Al-Komur and produced the four galaxies: sand and mud; some people from the ancient history of Al-Bijrawiyah, Al-Naqa', Kaboshiyah; some of them from the fringes of Al-Hambouti, Al-Mirmeedah, Jarab, and Al-Areef; and some from the Nile. They came from all passes of life and joy of days.

The Nile grants life to its banks and plains of Wadi Al-Hawad, of the eastern Al-Naqa' heights. From Al-Sadah Mountains and Fangol heights valleys come down. The eastern and western slopes meet at the tip of Nasri Island.

Nasri, Wad Abdullah, and the rest of islands are the connecting lines between the two Nile banks till modern bridges are built and hanging electric cableways (teleferiques) are run with tourists over Al-Komur's region.

Islands are inundated with water during the flood. They court the vast expansion of space and stars at the time of recession. Trees of Sesban, Al-Tarfa, and Al-Dahseer grow on heights of the islands. They loom after the flood and call for cultivation of Al-Hameesy and Al-Mugd.

The Nile's summer current builds and protects edges of the islands. The current calms down and turbidity of water is eliminated after the rage and boredom. The season of turmoil comes along and the flood swallows islands once more. Seasons pass by and migration to the Desert commences .

Immigration from the Nile is an expansion of fertility. Water flows out, trees planted, babies born, clouds embrace in space, valleys roar with rain storms that go down the slopes and irrigate the galaxies of Al-Komur with heavy floods one time from the Desert and another from the Nile.

The Nile floods and drives out inhabitants of the islands to the Desert. After sometime, drought and heat drive them back. In the journey back home the trouble of heat is eliminated. The arrow of the compass has become the instructor of the Nile to all directions to irrigate the Desert till it finally pours in the Nubia Lake.

The Nile's course and direction had changed. It entered a new region. Contours were not the only thing that changed, but concepts too so that facts, imaginations, and ideas between reality and fiction emerge.

Al-Komur acquired from nature the diversification; the lofty mountains, deep valleys, vast plains, and the great Nile flowing in the middle of Al-Komur. Mountains of Fangol, Al-Sadah, rising agricultural lands of Magboul, in addition to Khor (gorge) Mohyideen, Khoy, escarpment, and Wedy (small valley).

All these symbols meet below Al-Komur, unite with the Desert, Nile course, and deluge. Here appear the Arab features of Africa above the surface with two facts every year – desertification and inundation.

Around Al-Komur tributaries go down with rain water into the valley below the market and from there to the Nile's course. At the end of Abu Hawiyah valley in Khor Mohyideen, the desert sand covers a big part of the muddy land; and the Nile floods with mud to cover the sand.

Weapons of sand and mud spread on the public square of Al-Komur. They collide and unite since the beginning of creation. Valleys flow rapidly with floods like edges of swords to cover Al-Komur's land with mud. Nile waves surge to thrust fleeing sand and fold it.

Between spears and blades of swords Al-Komur shouts and calls "I am Al-Khumrah (Sudanese female fragrance composed of many perfumes left in a bottle for some days to ferment) from the oysters of the sea (Nile) and Al-Mahraibah (aromatic plant) from the Mountain's chest."

Example 2

Between reality and fiction

<u>The three stories</u>
1- Wad Al-Kateer (dcsert)
2- Saleem (Nilotic)
3-Anz -Alhambac (in between)

Desert is reality
Nilotic is Imagination
Between desert and Nile is the brown mixed of sand and muddy desert and Nile.

The Desert
Story Represent the Desert
Story of Wad Al-Kateer

Wad Kadak under his towing said the life full of devil, Wad Al-Kateer marriage from Jinn. We do not know what to do, just we pray to God to save us.

Wad Al-Kateer chose to live in the Desert and leave Al-Komur's community. He used to move with the big flock of sheep, rides a camel, and carries his luggage on a donkey. Wad Al-Kateer does not go down to Al-Komur except for shopping.

Do some people get married from female jinni? Does marital life become natural between them in interaction and sex?

He was known as Wad Al-Kateer, but nicknamed Abu .Ali. He was a member of Al-Tarjamiyah Village. He settled in the north western side of Al-Komur Village beside Um Zor after he surpassed forty five years of age and built a house for himself. He got married for the second time and started to make a family of human beings.

His first jinni wife was still chasing him. He alone could see her and no one else. After he married his second wife, the jinni wife vowed to retaliate. She destroyed everything he owned: the sheep and simpers, and used to come to him for a moment while he was awake or asleep.

He was a good and timid man who used to walk quietly and focus his sight on the ground. He used not to hug people when greeting them as Al-Komur's people do, but extend his hand for greeting as Bedouins. He was always ner to you with his heart at the moment of greeting. He used to smile slowly and was neither tall nor short. He was slim and slanted a little forward.

He did not like to tour Alkomur market. He used to sit leaning his back to one of the shop's pillars, survey with his sight all corners of the market and passers bye, stand abruptly, put his hands behind him, and walk out of the market.

Wad Al-Kateer used to perform light works in the market. He perfected painting houses from inside and transporting the colored soil in Eids (feasts). He had one goat for milk. The people of land and sea (Nile) were in the past days speaking about his big flocks of sheep.

Someone met him in the market, agreed with him to paint a room, and asked him about a color that inclines to orange. Wad Al-Kateer replied smilingly and precisely: "it is there in Fangol Mountains." He fetched that color, mixed it with water, and told the client that he would come to him after two days.

Wad Al-Kateer used to work quietly as if observing something going around him. I came with food at mid-day, put it before him, and asked him loudly:

"Oh, Abu Ali I want to ask you a question?"

Abu Ali: "Why not son! I don't mind."
And by his laughter I knew his
absolute approval. We talked together
about a fight that had occurred on last
Monday in the Animals Market.
He said to me: "But you have not
asked me?"
I said to him: "Is it true that you were
married to a jinni?"

He said: "Yes, by Allah my son.
Our time has now elapsed. That was
in the early days when I was young."
I asked: "how?"

"I was young, owned a lot of
animals, and used to shepherd them
alone in the countryside. A female
jinni used to come to me after
twilight. She was beautiful as normal
girls with a fair skin and black long
hair. Her fingers were thick and long
as if they had never touched
something. Her face was white,
cheeks bright, and a fistful thin waist.

She used to come to me from the
direction of the wind, perfumed with
Khumra (a Sudanese female fragrance
composed of a mixture of many

perfumes left in a bottle for some days to ferment), other sprinkling perfumes, had a smoke sauna of good-scented Talh and Shaf woods, massaged, and decorated hands and feet with black henna (camphire)."

He then cleared his throat and said: "Oh, boy her appointments were exact and known. She used to lie beside me and we were man and woman till the morning."

Groups of his tribe - inhabitants of Al-Tarjamiyah - tracked him down, waved to him to get down and live among people, and get married. They overcame him and convinced him.

He said: "The female jinni threatened me, vowed that if I left her she would show me woes in subsistence, children, and in myself. She wept and threatened when I left her. Every morning I found five of my animals dead. Gradually I lost them all."

He paused for a moment and said: "Before killing the animals, she used to utter some verses of poetry, I forgot them now! Any way with verses of the Holy Koran and religious and good people I managed to marry and live here. She used to come day after another, sit on the wall, and weep."

"Weeps at your house in Al-Komur?"

"Yes, at this well-known house of mine." He continues, you know once she came and sit Saleem come running around shouting announce that something wrong going on.

Saleem Nilotic but always helps the badwen.

Some people said Saleem is jin and devil too, some people said Saleem from the region between algadaref town east of Sudan and Atheubia, but Shabalel said he is kind mixed between human and crocodile, anyhow saleem Niolatic and the good lock always follow him rain and the plants come out a lot and quick.

Wad Al-Kateer had married a very tall and good physique polite woman. All neighbors spoke well about her. She knew rights of neighborhood, participated in occasions, and did her best to be nice with women in Al-Komur and neighboring villages.

Wad Al-Kateer and his wife were blessed with two boys and a daughter. The daughter married when she was eleven years old and left with her husband. The elder son Ali was fond of football. He and his younger brother made their best to help their father make the family happy.

The flock of animals started to drop one after another!! People knew the cause and they were no longer amazed. Rumors started to circulate in Al-Komur market.

Mohammed Wad Jubarah: "hey guys, have you heard of the tale of Wad Al-Kateer's goats and sheep?"
Hamad Rahamah: "May Allah help them?"

Ali Wad Siddiq lifted his right leg up on the couch of the coffee shop: "Oh folks, this female jinni will not leave them."

Faraj Wad Al-Huwar: "I think they have to look for a Faki "religious man" to release them of this misfortune."

Hamad Rahamah: "these folks deserve a help. This means we have to include them in the care and aid list."

Hamad and his group usually take care of the concerns and worries of inhabitants of the village.

The flock of sheep and goats gradually decreased and finally there was no goat to milk even for tea. Ali, the elder son, started frequently complaining from a fever that was quivering him. He died at the age of twenty, his brother followed suit in the same age, then the father and mother after some time.

The whole family tree fell off with its fruits in a cemetery beside the Nile. As fruits fall off a tree on a lake, small ripples come out on the surface. These circles grew wider and wider and finally fade away and fruits plunged deep in the lake.

Wad Al-Kateer house remained on the edge of Al-Komur Village. People abandoned it due to tales about the retaliating female jinni. When people pass by the house, they recite verses of the Holy Koran and curse jinn.

Butchers' noise grew louder in Souk Al-Komur and a hurly-burly outside the market mixed with bleats of goats in the Animals Market. Hajah bint Zainaldeen's house filled and emptied from both elder and young people. Students congregated around the sewing machine of Ali Wad Sineen and a number of farmers followed the merchant Ali Bashir for a loan and prepayments against future crops, as farming season was about to advent.

Floods of people entered from the five gates of the market. Al-Sir Wad Al-Ijaimi stood in the center of the market moving his head briskly and said: "where are these people going to?" he answered his question by saying: "yes, by Allah they are going to the Monday's

The Nile
Story represents The Nile

Saleem Al-Asaseem trace back to their ancestor Assoom. Their name is linked in Al-Komur village with the story of Saleem. I am not sure whether it is a legend, child stories, or a real one that happened some time ago.

The image of Saleem shadow Al-asaseem comes and goes in my mind. I have seen him in person and I now see him between reality and imagination. The tales neared the character of Saleem to reality. But undoubtedly he is a Nilotic reality!

Between dusk and evening Saleem comes out from the Nile with wet clothes. His face and shape both human. He walks on two legs and sometimes on four. His body covered with hair except his face, palms, and soles of his feet. Mosquitoes swarm around him. He drives them away with his hands. He was quiet, peaceful, and hurts no one. As a result he was called Saleem. He smiles exactly like a human being.

Al-Shabaleel's family says: he is a blend of human and ape. But members of Al-Asaseem say he works with them in farming. He is one of their slaves who works, eats, and drinks during the day. But in the dusk he goes down to the Nile, dives in it, and disappears all night.

Saleem is a Nile's creature who comes out in the morning and lives with Al-Asaseem in their farms. He practices one thing in disguise if he has the chance. He nurses on milk from goats of neighbors. Some people say he is a monkey. Elders swear that he is a human being who lives deep in the Nile.

The Kings - inhabitants of Al-Jabrab Village - say that Saleem appears in the dawn before sunrise and swims the Nile to Al-Asaseem land opposite to their waterwheels in Nasri Island.

Saleem disappeared for a long time after the migration of people from Nasri Island to Al-Komur, after Al-Tasab - the flood of 1946.

Abdul Majid Assoom built his house near Al-Kardab and Al-Shabaleel. Suddenly at sunset a cold wind blew from the Nile and Saleem, who grew older, appeared on two slim legs walking towards Al-Komur village. He sat down on a heap of stones between the house of Wad Malik and Wad Murad. Saleem smiled and turned about as if he found what he was searching for.

News of Saleem leaked and the people gathered. Hands extended to greet him. He extended his hands to greet two persons at a time. Abdul Majid Wad Assoom brought him food. Saleem left the group and started devouring the food. People took notice of him as he was weeping. They all went with him!

Hamad Wad Abdulraheem appeared protruding his chest out denying the news and looking for

Saleem among the gathering. He made his way through the people with both hands and saying: "hey folks, move aside please. Is it true that Saleem has come?"

Hamad sat on the ground, put his hands on his head and said: "I Witness that No God except Allah and that Mohammed is the Messenger of Allah. Hey folks, this is Saleem himself. Oh folks hail the good days of Nasri Island and our waterwheels." He also wept. Hamzah Al-Malek patted on Hamad's shoulder and said: "Hamad hush! Bygones are bygones and they will never come back."

At dawn and before sunrise, Saleem slowly got down the rock as if he came out of it and started walking towards the Nile. People followed him. He turned to them shyly, smiled, and kept his sight to the ground.

Neighboring villages rushed to see Saleem. Al-Hassaniyah Arabs came from the slopes of Fangol Mountains. Inhabitants of Al-Galah (Castle) rolled down from their houses into

Abu Hawiyah valley. Al-Ja'liyeen and Al-Jabrab rode their camels, horses, and donkeys followed by Al-Hawaweer. Inhabitants of Um Zor and Al-Tarjamiyah got down to Al-Komur.

All the people headed to the gap of the Desert. Men, women, and children climbed up Al-Tarad and gathered at its summit. Saleem said goodbye to them, retreated backwards, and descended into the Nile. The people requested him to come back. He started to dive and come up and finally disappeared.

People said at that mysterious night that the moon was full with a wide circle that overwhelmed all parts of the earth with light. Around its halo there were colored lines of yellow, blue, and green.

At that year the Nile flooded as never before till it reached the stones that Saleem sat on. And water entered the Alkomur market and inundated it. It was a year of blessings, abundance, and prosperity in Al-Komur market.

Saleem disappears for a long time and his arrival usually coincides with the last farmers' boat. He stays behind for some time and sits on the edge of Nile so that his body adapts to the air. News reaches Al-Komur and the people expect him. He sits on his usual rock. Abdul Majid Wad Assoom brings him food as usual. Saleem used to disappear and show up and with him blessings fill the market or disappear.

Saleem said goodbye to the people who were silent for a while then headed for their homes crossing the sands of the valley. And stories continued.

Hamad Wad Abdulraheem said: "Hey folks, let us go. Saleem has walked away. Our road is not the same."

Wad Kindi: "this sea (Nile) is all mysteries and enormities."

Wad Kadak hawked to continue talking: "Wad Kindi, haven't you seen Wad (son) of Al-Mulook (kings) who has struck the crocodile with a sickle?"

Wad Babiya interrupted him by saying: "he has not struck with a sickle only. But Wad Al-Mulook has fetched stones from Al-Jabrab Village. Once the crocodile comes out of water on the Island the boy storms him with stones."

Wad Kindi: "Aha, now the crocodile has snatched him."
All replied: "Yes, by Allah."

Wad Kindi ended the story by saying: "those who had seen him said when the crocodile grabbed him and went deep in the water, they said the hands that raised the boy were hands of a human being!!"Wad Kadak: "hey man, the creature that snatched the boy was doing that in retaliation."

The story reached an end when they entered the Village of Al-Komur and the roads branched at Al-Kardab's well. Hamad Wad Abdulraheem went eastwards, Wad Kindi westwards, Wad Kadak proceeded along towards the Vehicles Road, and the village roads swallowed the rest of men.

Between Desert and Nile

Story of Anez Al-Hambak
Fatima

Story of Anez Al-Hambak Fatima
Al-Hampack is inedible fruits come
out into ball shape, from Osher tree,
filled with air and seeds. It produces a
loud sound when pressure is applied.
Upon popping, the wind will scatter
the Oshry seeds with white winged.

Fatima was neither stout nor slim.
Her height was beautiful and her steps
were brisk, wide, and few if compared
to her height. She was black with soft
and long hair. When she speaks
everyone is able to hear her. She was
decent and wise.

She used not to turn about while
walking and when she has to she stops
and turns her whole body. All people
wish to talk to her. If she swears with
her two boys (Al-Bashir and Ali) it
means the truth and end.

Ali and Al-Bashir were two boys
among five girls. Three of these girls

lived in the urban and two in Al-Komur. President Nimeri hanged her grandson lieutenant colonel Ahmed Jubarah Al-Shala in Hashim Al-Ata's military coup.

Since I first saw her, she was wearing a white clean Thobe (a Sudanese sari-like cloth) and tying a red handkerchief around her neck. Those two colors increase the power and wisdom of her character and present her as a fighter and one of the granddaughters of the Arab famous female poet Al-Khansa.

Fatima used to mock but not laugh. Her speech among Al-Komur's community was constructive. She used to guide girls and glorify deeds of gallant men. When she loves something, she praises it very much and when she hates something she mutters with a low voice that increases her dignity and power of character.

Fatima also used to say her opinion clearly. One of her grandsons showed a desire to marry. She was not satisfied about the girl he wanted to marry. She told him after she murmured and a flood of words came out of her mouth: "Aha, when she sleeps, she slavers and when she tours the village, she stays long as if in a nap." He dismissed the idea of marrying that girl.

Fatima had a very beautiful daughter and there was a young handsome youth in Al-Komur called Wad Malik who married one of the daughters of Zainab bint (daughter) Hamzah who was a neighbor of Fatima. Fatima put the event in poetic words: "A'isha my daughter, who resembles the bottle on the shelf. Of bint Hamzah folks, the kite snatched her kaf (the sound of snatching). 'Kaf' is used here to rhyme with shelf)."

Fatima left for Khartoum to visit her children, for medical treatment, spend days of Eid (feast) among her married daughters and boys by moving from one to another. She was moving among them according to their requests. All requested her for her sweet talk and wisdom. At twelve o'clock (midday), a goat bleated at a corner of the courtyard. Fatima remembered Al-Komur and said to her daughter-in-law:

"Please my daughter; give this goat something to eat."
Her daughter-in-law: "he will come at two o'clock and will bring her clover with him (she meant her husband)."

Fatima murmured poetically: "Oh Allah, (Al-Zain) the Graceful, even the goat is waiting for (Athnain) the two o'clock."
Hamad Rahamah said to Mohammed Wad Jubarah: "have you heard of Anez (goat) Al-Hambak in Khartoum?"
Mohammed Jubarah: "the truth is that she does not mean the goat. She means herself."
Hamad Rahamah: "no, my brother, Fatima wants to be in her house; eats and drinks as she wishes."

The movement of Fatima among her daughters or sons-in-law takes her to her different present and makes her recalls the old memories written on the walls of her house in Al-Komur. She felt eager to go home and begged her daughters and sons to let her go home.

Her sons and daughters were eager to host her, but that was useless. She couldn't forget Al-Komur. It was impossible!

Fatima longed for Al-Komur - that precious pearl in a necklace of sand and water, covered with the Desert's color, and glowed with the Nile's blue into green and yellow!!

Poet Al-Jahoori said: "Oh how eager I am to the distant Al-Komur. Its fire increases sentiment. In the end I send greetings to Al-Turkey, the wooden board, Maseed (where he memorizes Holy Koran on a wooden board), and to everyone who asks about me. My greetings are sincere and they are all pure love. Soon I will see you Al-Komur. Oh Nasri, laugh for me a lot."

The heat of the sun dropped down and the Nile's breeze rolled up the last of the Desert's simoom (hot wind). It was five o'clock p.m. and a group of people were in front of Abbas's shop for different purposes. Some were waiting for buses and trucks from east and west.

Abbas Wad Al-Hidai stood up to fill the ewer from the array of large jars in front of the shop. Rolled up his Damoriyah (cotton) shirt with his thumb and the forefinger to the middle of his chest and said about the heat: "thank Allah, He cooled it a little! It was about to swallow us."

In front of the shop there were also women from Hajer Al-Tair (mount of birds) Village came to offer their condolences in Al-Kumur and waiting for the bus coming from Shandi. School pupils were smoking and discussing the football match between Hilal (Crescent) and Mireekh (Mars) teams.

Elders were enjoying listening to the radio where Dr. Abdullah Al-Tayyeb was explaining the Sura (chapter of the Holy Koran) of Al-

Nazea't while Sheikh Siddiq Ahmed Hamdoon was reciting. Girls around the well were filling their tins hurriedly so that bus passengers could not see them.

The bus stopped as an iron cage and opened its doors and her Thobe (a Sudanese sari-like cloth) flapped like the wings of a caged bird finally released. Fatima got down of the bus as a drowning person rescued by waves that drove him to the Desert's sand.

Fatima said: "Al-Komur is the land of security." And added: "I ask Allah forgiveness, salute to you men." All were in front of Abbas's shop.

Abbas said: "hello my aunt Fatima, how are the folks there in Khartum?"

Fatima: "thank Allah, they are all right. Come in the shop and give me a pound of sesame oil in a nylon bag." Then she uttered a couple of words only: "how is Al-Komur?"

Abbas: "secure and safe."

The oil bag swung in her hand, she grabbed it with two fingers, and went out of the shop.

Fatima: "bye, may Allah take care of you!"

With wide strides she passed over the threshold, easily forgot the trouble of the journey, and stretched her body in the street heading towards her house with the hand bag on her left hand and the oil bag on the right.

After passing the corner of the shop, a cold wind of the shadow, she knew best, touched her face. It was the fragrance of homeland. She muttered the word of Al-Komur.

The keys of the outer door, room, and other keys were all tied to her Thobe (a Sudanese sari-like cloth). She attacked the outer door. The goats jubilated a lot in the house of her daughter Faraheen (means double joy) and bleated high heralding her arrival. What amazing was that the goats did not see Fatima, but something happened!

Fatima stretched her tall physique in the middle of the courtyard and inspected its corners. The array of large water jars was empty for a long time. She headed towards the room, opened the door, looked upwards more than downwards, and counted important things hanging on the ceiling. The rain did not destroy them.

Fatima lifted Al-Angaraib (wooden bed) to her right side and hugged the pillows as if she was hugging a deer and beloved person. The bed was rectangular shaped with high legs. It becomes a trapezium when you move it, but returns back to the rectangular shape when it settles down on the ground. Its legs were not decorated with geometrical shapes only, but also with time old stories.

Fatima got into the house again and looked at the packs of the rolled Damour (cotton clothes) and straw mats tied with ropes made by Al-Tarshan (the deaf). How many straw mats, ropes, cushions have worn out and the bed is still there!! She changed its left leg and tied another with a strip of a cow's hide.

She spread the straw mat and fetched an oil-smeared pillow. She took the blue two-surface table. The lower surface of the table was made of one piece of wood where she put her snuff box. She poured the oil in a pot, changed her clothes, poured oil on her hands and started anointing her body.

The outer door moved and a ten years old girl came in after hearing the movement in the house. "My grandmother has arrived!" She returned back hurriedly from one house to another. "Al-Busharah (prize for the good news) Al-Busharah, my grandmother has arrived." News spread with the evening dreams.

Her daughter Faraheen stretched out her neck over the neighbors' wall and told her other sister. Her sister called her neighbor and thus news spread farther. The doors moved, goats bleated, and her daughter came in rushing and pulling half of her thobe (Sudanese sari-like cloth) on the ground. A throng of children were jumping in the middle of the courtyard with candy papers flying up from their hands. "My grandmother has arrived! My grandmother has arrived!"

The girls with successive voices: " how are you, mother?" they came towards her with their bosoms and hands opened to hug her. They took turn in hugging and greeting her.

Faraheen to her mother: "you have opened the door and took out the bed? You are also anointing!"
Fatima poetically: "hey girls, the oil is mine and the house is mine too. I am free to do with them. No Karkabah (noise) and no one will say I stained the Martabah (the mattress)."

One of her granddaughters slept at her feet, behind her there was a child, and another granddaughter of her second daughter was on the other bed. Nevertheless, Fatima slept profoundly.

Fatima was happy with her dreams, swam with Ursa Minor and Major (Little and Great Bears), wandered with ostriches, chased horses, lead the galaxy road fearing scorpions, and the aster came to her with the morning tea.

All around her laughed. In that winter day news spread farther in Al-Komur as a light rain. Al-Haid told Al-Hawad, Al-Na'oom heard, and news spread.

Echoes of Fatima's story overwhelmed Fangol, Al-Azozab, Al-Ja'liyeen Village, Al-Jabrab, Al-Tarjamiyah, and Galat (Castle) of Al-Bakriyah. When they mention her name, they all remember her past tales and end saying: "thank Allah, she came safe."

Hamdeen narrates to the gathering of Al-Tarjamiyah one of Fatima's tales, and Taiallah imitates her voice and gait. They all laughed and one of them said: "hey man thank Allah, she came safe." In Um Zor the girls of Al-

Sha'it also said: "thank Allah, she came safe."

Hamad Rahamah and Mohammed Jubarah entered the coffee shop and restaurant of Hasabalrasool in Souk Al-Komur for breakfast.

Hamad: "Please two dishes of beans with more oil on them."

Hasabalrasool: "oil of Anez (goat) Al-Hambak."

They all laughed and quoted Fatima's words:

"The oil is mine and the house is mine too. I am free to do with them. No Karkabah (noise) and no one will say I stained the Martabah (the mattress).

I write about Al-Komur, as it is built in the region of natural struggle, between the Nile and the Desert. The Nile floods annually, overwhelms its basin, and covers sands. Valleys flow carrying sands from the Desert's heights to overflow the Nile basin. The area below Al-Komur witnesses a battle between alluvium and sand. As a result Al-Komur's land divides into the soil of the Nile and soil of the Desert.

The clear division of soil does not prevent it from advancing and mixing. The Nile floods with its armies to inundate the soil. Sands develop barricades so that Al-Komur's region stands between the Nile's army and Desert's "Janjaweed" (a group of looters in Darfur's conflict in western Sudan).

The battlefield is equally divided down the valley - from west to east - between the two giants into four names i.e. two for each. They are: Al-Karo and Abu Hawiyah, Um Bagarah, and Abu Jamal anchorage.

The two soils desert and Nile mix and become red as clotted blood of many wars. They also become green and yellow. Sometimes only a thin thread separates between them from becoming sand or mud.

Conclusion

Desert and Nile is the school of analysis and criticism apply on human nature and art, literature poem and picture. Desrt and Nile is a resorces for art criticism. The valleys from the natural desert gaps made and contributed in building the artificial gaps, and how valleys extended their deposits into the Nile in the form of sand and island.

In conclusion, this shows how deserts and mountains form in the Nile; and how aquatic and ambitious animals follow desert sands and mountains into the Nile water. Tracking living things in Al-komur region- in land and water –has the nature of the Nile, Desert and mountain. They are indications to the Sudanese cultural affiliation. (Cataract is the mountain, the sand from the desert make the island, both surrounded by the Nile River water). In conclusion, do you consider yourself an artist?

Some inspire most about knowing that art is everywhere and how art has developed over the years. Art in the beginning were simple pictures on the walls, little paintings of grass, and on the ground it was so different. What makes it different now? The big difference is the creativity and the knowledge and the science that we have. Now art is an idea, a creative story. There are sculptures, paintings, songs and CDs, that are being revolutionized into a new form of art.

Part (7)
Analysis workshop and Suggest
reading and Conclusion

Analysis workshop
Practice and Quiz.

1-Story of Anz –Alhambac means:

A-Desert
B- Nile
C- Brown area
D- Ocean

2- Wad-Alcatar represent:-

A- The Nile River
B- The middle area
C- Desert
D- Island

3- Story of Saleem is:

A- The Nile River
B- The desert
C- Brown
D- Mountain

4- Community Art doing by:-

A- Individual
B- Company or group of people
C- By accident

D- Brush

5- You are Artist because:-

A- You draw and paint
B- Practice Art sometime
C- Only in the school
D- You practice Art every Day.

Suggest reading

Looking at art in the world through different perspective

The Art's Government
The Art's Government
There are six types of Art, six minister
fewer than six ministers.

The president office
Treasure and value
The economy and communication,
information and technology

- The president and ministry of treasure and value. Value comes

out from the six types of arts.

The difference between creativity and human-made is that creativity is the beginning that comes out from nothing but, makeup is hand-made, because resources exist, so the human make up and the God creator.

Computers such as laptops, tablets and cellphones will be used to help people and certain people will be in charge of creating specifically engineered technology like batteries with a longer lasting life and walk talkies to connect overseas.

The electric solar system it is makeup by human but come out from the sun created by God.

The six ministries is environment and minsters are watcher for communication, makeup and development. The products are parts of the six types of arts: the office of treasure and value the president and the six minister under the system of three; technology, announcement and information disseminated between six governments, preachers and art.

1-**Ministry of Visual** and visual resources of three dimensions, any image surrounded and possible to go around it (natural, handmade or machine product): like building, cars, furniture, craft and sculptures or any three dimensional. They will build

2-**Ministery of intellectual** and intellectual resources: Education and culture bookbinding publishing (information television radio newspapers).

4-**Ministry of fashion,** and fashion resources; factory of fabric and design, beauty supply (any new fashion show on human body, female or male dressing, animals or even on building).

4-**Ministry of physical** and physical resources; Military, Police, security and sports (soccer, basketball wrestling, dancing, acting, football and all type of sport and human's body movement. Include health (The victory of equipment's of medical and pharmacies).

5-**Ministry of Technology**, and technological resources; First of all electric from different resources (sun, cataract) the factory of technological products (modern and postmodern transportation) (Photography, cinema, cinematography, television, video, computer, cd's, laptop, I pat, telecom, home phone, cellphone.

6-**Ministry of Natural,** and natural resources; human, social life, animals and natural transportation, forest, trees, food, Geographic weather Land Ocean, rain, rivers, dames sky, ground; mountain, hill, stone, sandy stone, desert and Nile.

If the government applies money and technology on each part and follow up the devolvement, with a good relationship with neighbors and wide more around, the country will go fast. The president term is six years, one year attention to each part, no more term.

Conclusion

Art Ideas:-

Art is very special; because art is everywhere you go. I do not think I am an artist, but once I figure out Iam getting dress, working, swimming, and drawing, that's where the true artist comes in. Art is very special to me; because every time I play outside at the park or watching a soccer game in the stadium, I make sure that art is everywhere.

Painting on paper canvas and even the human body is a creative art while walking or talking, and because using painting and drawing materials to be creative, with all of the art work that can be combined together. Through the life of a human, learning all of the techniques of an artist can even help you become an artist.

From this book; the readers will learn six types of art which they never knew before, some may actually know parts of them. Life is creative; nature itself is within beauty, texture, and all kinds of things from any corner is art.

once finished read this book I feel satisfied and happy of what I learned about art.

Everyone would love to go out, into the open world, to discover new art visually or intellectually in our life journey. Art is wherever because of the materials and the usage items or images of them. Most people don't really notice because writing and explanation about art is not as big as it was before. It was really important back in the Stone Age and during the renaissance to the postmodern.

Everyone uses art every day, due to the technology that has covered our life. In the last twenty years, using a cell phone to call, or computers to type, is using intellectual and technology art in the same way. Never get noticed and realized, until you look up to the materials that was used by artists, to find out about the ancient art in our worlds history.

That is not enough to practically using the art, but supposed to know about history and the time line when that happened. Say I am an artist, because I use my phone and other technological devices every day, but how the home developed from telephones to home phones to cellphones and we do not know what will happen about tomorrow from the researches and the new knowledge.

A student said to his friend: "I am drawing while I'm bored in one of my activities, if I need to occupy my time for whatever reason; I would pull out a book or sketch pad and start drawing anything that comes to mind like exercise sports or nature's environment.

His friend answered: "So anything you do to express yourself, goes on paper. You express how you feel around your surroundings, even playing games."

Sports acts or dancing is certain types of arts, we mainly know about. Before reading this book, it didn't necessarily make me appreciate art due to the fact that it was something that I had always harbored admiration for, but it did ignite inspiration in which I already had passion for, which motivates me to do what I want to do in my everyday life, with my artistic eyes. This book is more than anything that has made me fall in love with the idea of art again.

The idea was something that brought me comfort, and allowed me to feel more relatable to people who are newly exposed to what art represents in full. Now I feel more comfortable with expressing my ideas of art with those now learning about it, because now the idea and images is more different.

Now the environment is a little greater than an amateur's perspective, now that they have been enlightened to. By spending the knowledge of art, it only makes way for one's imagination to run wild in the most positive sense. Say I am an artist because I am a master of creativity, for all of my thoughts related to art are filled with passion.

From this book, I learned that everything could consider art in some way. Before reading this book, I would not have considered most things as art. However, I learned that there are six types of art; which they are visual, intellectual, physical, fashion, technology, and natural.

When I look up in the sky, I try to form shapes on the constellation stars. Whenever I dress myself, I see art because I am matching colors and wearing different styles of clothes. Whenever playing soccer with my friends, I see myself an artist. We are all artists.

We are all artists because we create art with our talents. Without art, the world would be black and white. Artists painted our life by happiness, such as the way a person dance, sing, or even draw? Artists create and we portrait our inside images, based off how we look, smell, talk, act. We are part of art ourselves. Without artist, art wouldn't exist.

Am I an Artist? I consider myself an artist, after I reviewed this book. To being an artist takes more than just opening notebooks of sketch paper and opening your mind. In order to be an artist, you need to understand that you are an artist yourself, and everything you do is art. When I am writing on a piece of paper, that is consider type of intellectual art, similar to physical arts.

One day I am physical outside riding my bike, looking around in the park, to be just in the atmosphere that is art also. We can find that; knowing everything we do is art and inspire everything you do is art and we are an artist. Art is very where and important in our life. This book taught a lot of things and made any one realize that proud to say I am an artist.

Waking up in the morning and choose warring clothes or decorating the room is art, and just realizing playing sports is an art and I realized when I did my project on how soccer can be a part of art, I never saw it that way. Art is in our lives and we don't even realize. One of the student wondering and answered; I never saw it that way.

I realized how art is important in our lives and the way we live, we live in art. Thank you the author for such a good book and the real meaning of art. That inspire us to do what we want to do and consider art. Knowing that everything I do art is the most motivating thing in the world. All you need is creativity and motivation to do something and you are considering an artist. So yes, to answer the question I am an artist.

Over this entire book is great I learn a lot of things; I didn't think I would learn. Coming into art, I thought art when we would be trying to learn to draw. I was happy to learn that art wasn't just about drawing that there is way more to art. Before I read this book I would have never thought that there are six type of art. I thought that art meant art, I am glad to know the true meaning of art now from this book.

Do you really consider yourself an artist? Yes, you do but in some cases, you really wouldn't. Because you know how to classify yourself as an artist, you might be able to add music taste as an artistic trait. However since music is an intellectual art, you truly appreciating it is appreciating art.

1-Books physically or on line:-
-Alkomur market
-Notes; desert and Nile

2-Nubian north of Sudan
-pg.: 48 to 57 back to illustration pg…
Art is an idea….
-Pg.: 58 to 65

3-The shadow of Saleem
-Reading from pg. 21 to 35

4-Internet:-
-Free research

5-The vocabulary:-
-Visual art
-Tow dimension and three dimension

Works Cited

Bio-Tec. Environmental Effects of plastic pollution. Bio-Tec Environmental. 2017. https://hyperallergic.com http://ww.bbc.com/news/magazine-27442625 (Laurence Knight)(May 14th, 2014) www.goecopure.com/environmental-effects-of - plastic- poiiution.aspx>

Clean water Action. The problem of marine ploastic pollution. Clean Water. Action. 2017. http://www.Clean water.org/problem-marine –plastic- pollution>

Creek life.Six Reasons why plastic is bad for the Environment. Creek life. 2013 http://creeklife.com/blog/six-reasons-why-plastic-is bad for the environment/

Ecology Center. AdvgerseHeath Effects of Plastic. EcolgyCenter.2012 https://ecologycenter. .org/factsheets/adverse-health-effect-of-plastic/

Knoblauch, Jessica. Plastic Not-so-Fantastic: How the Versatile Material

harms the Environment and Human Health. Scientific America.2009
https://WWW.sciantificamericaan.com /article/plastic-not-so-fantastic/
Citation
www.thoughtco.com- use of plastic 820359
https://en.wiipeia.org/wiki/plastic
plastepedia.co.uk-A brief history of plastics

Made in the USA
Coppell, TX
15 September 2021

62389879R00125